M000222742

MESSENGERS
OF
GOD

MESSENGERS

OF
GOD

A JEWISH PROPHETS
WHO'S WHO

RONALD H. ISAACS

JASON ARONSON INC.
Northvale, New Jersey
Jerusalem

This book was set in 12 pt. Corona by Alabama Book Composition of Deatsville, Alabama.

Library of Congress Cataloging-in-Publication Data

Isaacs, Ronald H.
    Messengers of God : a Jewish prophets' who's who / by Ronald H. Isaacs.
        p.   cm.
    Includes bibliographical references.
    ISBN 0-7657-9998-7 (alk. paper)
    1. Bible. O.T. Prophets—Criticism, interpretation, etc.
    2. Prophecy—Judaism. 3. Prophets in rabbinical literature.
    4. Judaism—Liturgy. I. Title.
    224'.06—dc21   97-33198

Manufactured in the United States of America. Jason Aronson Inc. offers books and cassettes. For information and catalog write to Jason Aronson Inc., 230 Livingston Street, Northvale, New Jersey 07647.

For my son Zachary,
whose namesake
is the Prophet Zechariah

Contents

Contents   xi

I

Who and What
Are Prophets

1

Early Prophets in the Bible

A variety of figures in the Bible were referred to as prophets. Abraham, the first Hebrew, was called a prophet: "You must restore the man's wife—since he is a prophet" (Genesis 20:7).

Moses was twice called a prophet in the Bible: "God will raise up for you a prophet from among your own people like myself. And you shall heed him" (Deuteronomy 18:15); and "Never again did there arise in Israel a prophet like Moses, who God singled out, face to face . . ." (Deuteronomy 34:10).

According to the Book of Deuteronomy, the origin of the office of prophecy is rooted in the experience at Mount Sinai. Since the Israelites were afraid of receiving God's word directly in a public theophany, they requested that Moses "go closer . . . and hear all that God says, and tell it to the people" (Deuteronomy 5:27). This is corroborated by the following personal description of Moses: "I stood between God and you at that time to convey God's word to you, for you were afraid of the fire and did not go up to the mountain" (Deuteronomy 5:5).

Thus, Moses became the spokesperson of God to the people. Although Moses certainly spoke for God in a special way, he is still considered more a facilitator in the dissemination of God's Law and a leader of the Israelites, rather than a prophet in the traditional sense.

The word *prophet* has had a variety of meanings during different periods of Jewish history. Some of the earliest prophets in the Bible are referred to by four different names in Hebrew: *chozeh* and *ro'eh*, both meaning a "seer"; *ish ha'Elohim*, "man of God"; and *navi*, "prophet." A seer was a person who possessed the ability to foretell the future and to reveal information that was concealed from ordinary human beings. The term *ro'eh* is first applied to Samuel in 1 Samuel 9, when Saul, in search of his father's donkeys, seeks the aid of the seer Samuel and is even prepared to pay a fee of one-quarter of a *shekel*. Samuel, who in this narrative (1 Samuel 9:6) is also called a "man of God" and who had been previously informed by God of Saul's arrival, provides the necessary information and, in addition, anoints Saul the King of Israel. He then informs Saul of the events that are about to befall him on his way home, including the fact that he will meet a band of prophets. King Saul himself, upon the urging of Samuel the Priest, is described (1 Samuel 10:5–11) as having participated in a band of roving *nevi'im*. In other parts of the Bible there are also references to groups of prophets, often prophesying in a state of high emotional frenzy. Such prophetic groups were often consulted for advice and asked to deliver oracles in the name of God.

The title *chozeh* is first applied to Gad in 2 Samuel 24:11, where Gad is called the *chozeh* of David. In essence, Gad was one of a number of court prophets who served the king. He was not a literary prophet but a diviner, a visionary of sorts, who perhaps had some special power and appeared to speak in God's name. He was kept in the king's court and used to consult oracles or to make divinations, an especially important task before a major military campaign. Other court prophets were Asaph, Heman, and Jeduthun, who could prophesy with lyres, harps, and cymbals (1 Chronicles 25:1).

These early prophets certainly played a role in the communal affairs of the Israelites. They had a number of common characteristics, such as having the ability to make predictions about the future, functioning as part of a guild, employing musical accompaniment to induce or heighten their frenzy, and usually (unlike the literary prophets) telling the people what they wanted to hear.

On occasion these early prophets showed more independence and a great deal of courage. For instance, Elijah the Prophet's condemnation of King Ahab, who had a temple built to the pagan god Baal (1 Kings 21), was an act of great courage on his part. Clearly, he risked his life in standing up for what he believed to be a desecration to God. Elisha, Elijah's faithful servant, was also faithful to the legacy of his master Elijah. He was forceful and often carried out his prophetic mission to perfection, even when it involved deep internal conflicts.

Sometimes the early prophets were even paid for their work. This would have been unthinkable for one of the classical literary prophets. Amos (7:14) denied that he was a prophet by profession. The Prophet Micah (2:6) disdained prophets who made a living by prophecy. They never reached the prominent stature of the great major and minor literary prophets, whose mission always consisted of reproving the people in an attempt to save them from destruction.

2

Women Prophets

Five women are called "prophetesses" in the Bible. Three of them, Deborah, Huldah, and Noadiah, actually spoke in the name of God, but only Deborah and Huldah had their words recorded in the Bible. Of the remaining two, one was never identified by name and the other never prophesied.

Deborah, unlike other great women in the Bible who are either married to a great man or related to one, stands exclusively on her own merits. She is referred to as both a military leader and as a prophetess. Together with Barak, she led the Israelites to a victorious battle against the Canaanites, memorializing the victory in the famous "Song of Deborah," recorded in chapters four and five of the Book of Judges. A special Sabbath, known as the Sabbath of the Song, was instituted by the rabbis; it recalls the Exodus from Egypt and on it we read the famous Song of Moses (Exodus, chapter 15). On that very same Sabbath, Deborah's Song of Thanksgiving is recited as the prophetic reading (i.e., the *Haftarah*) of that day, thus preserving its memory each and every year.

Huldah lived during the last years of the Judean monarchy, some five hundred years after Deborah. She predicts, in the Second Book of Kings, the destruction of the Kingdom of Judah.

Mention is made in the Book of Isaiah (8:3) of the wife of the Prophet Isaiah, who bore him a son: "I was intimate with the prophetess, and she conceived and bore a son." There is no explanation given in the book for her title as prophetess.

Noadiah, sometimes referred to as the "false prophetess," is mentioned in the Book of Nehemiah (6:12–14) as one of a group of people who were opposed to his activities in the holy city of Jerusalem.

Finally, Miriam, the sister of Aaron and Moses, received the title of prophetess in Exodus 15:20 upon her leading the women in song and dance, with timbrels in hand, after the Israelites crossed the Red Sea.

Compared to their male counterparts, these women did not function as prophets in the traditional sense. They did not preach lengthy messages nor did they have visions and dreams with which to help them predict future events for the Jewish people.

3

False Prophets

If one were to have lived in biblical times, how could one have been certain that a person who said he was a prophet was authentic? The description in the Bible of the Israelite prophets is preceded by a stern and detailed denunciation of any dealings with people who attempted to learn the future and prophesy by using means such as augury and sorcery rather than by direct communication from God. Practitioners of the science of divination (which includes those who use astrology, charms, incantations, and magic) were well-known in the Ancient Near East. Because of divination's popularity, the Bible strongly cautioned against its use. For example, the Book of Leviticus (19:31) warns: "Do not turn to ghosts to inquire of familiar spirits." One of the most comprehensive prohibitions occurs in Deuteronomy 18:10–11: "Let no one among you be found who consigns his son or daughter to the fire, or who is an auger, a soothsayer, a diviner, a sorcerer or one who casts spells, or who consults ghosts or familiar spirits, or who inquires of the dead. Such a person that does these things is an abomination to God . . ." This injunction is leveled mainly against the divinatory practices of the Canaanites, who rely too much on their own human skill to penetrate the Divine mysteries. Thus, divination is pagan in origin, and its practitioners continue to be linked in various Books of the Prophets to false prophets.

Interestingly, there is no Hebrew term in the Bible for a false prophet. Both false and true ones were simply called *nevi'im*—"prophets." The Book of Deuteronomy attempts to provide criteria to distinguish true from false prophets immediately following its anti-divination statements, saying that "any prophet who presumes to speak in God's name an oracle which God did not command or speaks in the name of other gods, that prophet shall die. And should you ask yourselves, 'How can we know that the oracle was not spoken by God?' . . . if the prophet speaks in the name of God and the oracle does not come true, that oracle was not spoken by God . . ." (Deuteronomy 18:20–22). In other words, the test of a true prophet is whether the prediction does or does not come true.

The next chapter will describe the so-called literary prophets, whose words filled entire books. Of all of the major prophets, the Prophet Jeremiah is the most consistent in speaking with the intent to combat false prophecy. In the twenty-third chapter of his book, in recognizing Hananiah as a false prophet, Jeremiah identifies three characteristics of the false prophet:

1. Those who have dreams and mislead people;
2. Those who "steal" God's words and pretend that they have direct revelation; and
3. Those who concoct their own oracles and pass them off as prophecy.

A person's technical expertise on predicting the future is not, and can never be, true prophecy. For prophecy to be authentic, the initiative must be taken entirely by God, Who communicates intentions through visions and Who cannot be coerced by any humanly devised means, no matter how clever, to reveal His designs.

4

Literary Prophets

The second section of the *Tanakh*, the Hebrew Bible, is called *Neviim*, "The Prophets." It commences with the era when the Judges ruled Israel. It then traces the history of Israel's kings, commencing with Saul, and concludes with the return of the Babylonian exile. But most importantly, this division of the Bible deals with the teachings of the great literary prophets of Israel who brought the words of God to an often erring people. Isaiah, Jeremiah, and Ezekiel were the so-called Major Prophets, because of the lengthy books named after them. Hosea, Joel, Amos, Obadiah, Jonah, Micah, Nachum, Habakkuk, Zephaniah, Haggai, Zechariah, and Malachi comprised the so-called Minor Prophets. Each of these latter prophets has a much smaller book named after him.

The prophets were persons chosen by God and dedicated to God's service. They were called to their mission during a time of political and social crisis in the community, and their task was to warn and counsel the Israelite people, having foreseen the outcome of various national crises as well as the evil practices of the people. Fearlessly, they criticized the morality and ethics of their era and taught a nobler way of living.

The following is a brief summary of the literary prophets (including the non-literary prophets Elijah and Elisha), in chronological order according to the time in which they lived. All the dates are before the Common Era:

874–840 **Elijah,** champion of God against Baal, or idol-worship. He opposed Jezebel, the foreign wife of King Ahab, who introduced idol-worship.

840–8   **Elisha,** successor of Elijah. He played an important role in the revolution against Ahab.

785   **Jonah** made his famous trip to Nineveh to prophesy its doom. At first he tried to run away from God, then he was swallowed by a huge fish.

780–740 **Amos,** the prophet of justice, preached the restoration and future glory of the kingdom of King David.

750–722 **Hosea** was the prophet of love and forgiveness. His message contained the doctrine of a universal God for all of the nations.

738–700 **Isaiah,** the statesman prophet, described the ideal state and the golden age of human beings. In his book, the collective Israel was described as a suffering servant (chapter 53).

735–700 Micah urged every person to do justly, love mercy, and walk humbly with God.

630–623 Zephaniah lived in the days of King Josiah's reformation. He strongly condemned the idolatrous nations and threatened God's impending judgment.

625–608 Nachum foretold the destruction of Sennacherib's army.

626–586 Jeremiah was the prophet of sorrow and doom. He predicted the destruction of the Jerusalem Temple.

600–590 Habbakuk preached the message of faith. God's punishment of Israel teaches the lesson that "the righteous shall live by faith."

586 Obadiah's book is only one single chapter, the shortest of all of the literary prophets. It is directed against Israel's enemy, the nation of Edom.

597–571 Ezekiel was the leader and comforter of the Israelites while they were in Babylonian exile. He laid the foundation for the Jewish religion as we know it today.

586–534 Daniel, the prophet of exile, foretold the restoration of Israel and the coming of God's universal kingdom.

520–516 **Haggai** returned to Palestine from Babylonia and urged the rebuilding of the Temple that stood in Jerusalem.

445–432 **Malachi** prophesied that Elijah would announce the coming of God's Messiah. His is the last book in the canon of the prophets.

400   **Joel.** His time of activity is uncertain. He lived during a plague of locusts, which he interpreted to be God's Divine justice.

5

Principles of Jewish Prophecy

The institution of Jewish prophecy was founded on the basic premise that God makes His will known to certain chosen individuals in successive generations. Called prophets, they are described in their books as charismatic people endowed with the Divine gift of both receiving and imparting the message of revelation. Prophets were elected by God and were irresistibly compelled to deliver God's message and impart God's Will, even if they personally disagreed with it.

Questions concerning prophecy have abounded throughout the ages. People have always wanted to know how God spoke to the prophets and how they were able to hear. Did they have to train themselves to hear God's voice? Were they endowed with a separate faculty, a special sense?

In the Bible, we are told that God frequently speaks to people. For instance, the verse "God spoke to Moses, saying" appears numerous times in the Five Books of Moses and almost invariably initiates the dialogue between God and Moses.

God, too, first spoke to the prophets, and they do not speak until and unless God first addresses them. God was always seeking out people to be His prophets; the prophets never grasped after God.

The great prophets of Israel heard and perceived God everywhere—in the winds, in the rushing waters, in the flames of fire, and in the sands of the wilderness. The truth, however, is that what they heard continues to elude all scientific inquiry. It is impossible to pierce its mystery, for we have only received in their writings the stories of what happened to them—what they heard, what they saw, how they felt, and how they reacted.

In the Book of Kings, the Prophet Elijah finds himself atop a mountain. There, he experiences fire, earthquake, and wind, but the Bible tells us that God was not in all of these natural phenomena. Rather, we are told that God is to be found in the still small voice (1 Kings 19:12). It is here that Elijah learned the importance of silence and listening.

Prophets had many attributes in common. The prophets of Israel appear to share these characteristics:

1. Generally speaking, prophets were loners, solitary figures who did not have many close friends. Since their predictions generally involved something that the people did not want to hear, they were quite unpopular and were frequently denounced by the people whose lives they tried to change. This often caused them a great deal of personal pain. Interestingly, at first none of the prophets really wanted to be prophets. Many of

them present excuses to God as to why they are unworthy of the task. Ultimately, though, once God has made His decision, it is impossible for a prophet to shirk his duty.

2. Prophets always arose during times of social and political crisis. They often saw their prophecy in a dream or a night vision or during the day while in a trance.

3. All authentic prophets were able to correctly predict what would happen to the people of Israel. Their predictions were not grounded in sorcery or divination but on the information provided to them by God or His angels.

4. Prophets often presented their messages in the form of allegories or parables. The interpretation of these would be quickly implanted in the prophet's mind, and thus the prophet would be able to explain their meaning.

5. Prophecy was frequently a traumatic experience. The prophet's limbs often trembled and their bodies became faint.

6. The literary prophets had their words written down in books that have been named after them. Some had scribes or secretaries to whom they dictated their messages.

7. The words of the prophets were often very expressive, and the poetic beauty of their language majestic. Thus, the words of the prophets are able

to elicit a great deal of emotion on the part of the reader.

8. Often, one of the prophet's tasks was to soothe and comfort and despondent Israelite people. After the commemoration of the Fast of the Ninth of *Av*, seven prophetic portions, known as the "*Haftarot* of Consolation," are read each successive Saturday morning at Sabbath services.

9. Many of the things that horrified the prophets in their time (e.g., the wealthy neglecting the poor, people performing ritual rotely, without feeling, and so forth) continue to manifest themselves today in life's daily occurrences.

10. Prophets were often angered by people who meticulously observed Jewish ritual and observance while they ignored the ethical and moral concerns of society, such as the plight of the poor and the hungry.

11. Among the prophetic messages to the people was that of a God Who allows for second chances through the process of repenting for one's transgressions.

12. Many of the prophets preached the importance of being ethical and moral.

13. Prophets do not volunteer for their mission. The mission is forced upon them by Divine authority, and they have no choice but to accept their prophetic duty.

14. Revelation and God's word came upon the prophets as a surprise, and they were usually startled at that which they heard.

15. Prophets were iconoclasts, challenging the apparently holy and revered.

16. Prophets write using emotional and imaginative language, poetic and artistic in form. Their words are often stern and stinging, but they also bring consolation, promise, and the hope of reconciliation. Generally, they begin with a message of doom and end with a message of promise and hope.

17. The fundamental experience of the prophet is a fellowship with the feelings of God.

6

After Prophecy: The *Bat Kol*

With the deaths of the Prophets Malachi, Zechariah, and Haggai in the fifth century before the Common Era, the days of the classical literary prophets came to an end. According to rabbinic tradition, the *bat kol*, a heavenly voice, became God's sole mechanism of revealing His will to human beings after the cessation of prophecy (Talmud, *Yoma* 9b). The rabbis believed that the *bat kol* was already heard during biblical times. For instance, in the Talmud (*Makkot* 23b) they believed that it was heard to proclaim Tamar's innocence as well as to validate Solomon's judgment in awarding the child to the true mother. In the *Midrash*, a *bat kol* tells Moses that God will attend his burial.

The *bat kol* was sometimes said to give heavenly approval to Jewish legal decisions, although its pronouncements were not necessarily accepted.

II

Talmudic Views of Prophecy

7

Overview

As is quite typical of the Talmud, there is no systematic discourse on the nature of prophecy given by any of the talmudic authorities. Two main principles do emerge that are most salient. The first is that Moses was the "master of all of the prophets" and that there was no prophet after him who was as capable at penetrating the nature of God Himself, communicating with the Divine, and receiving God's message with great clarity while still in total possession of his faculties. The rabbinic proof text for this observation is Numbers 12:6–8, in which God comes down in a pillar of cloud and speaks to Aaron and Miriam with words that distinguish Moses from the other prophets: "Hear now My words: if there be a prophet among you, I the Lord do make Myself known unto him in a vision. I do speak with him in a dream. My servant Moses is not so; he is trusted in all My house. With him do I speak mouth to mouth, even manifestly, and not in riddles, and he beholds the likeness of God."

This concept is further elaborated upon in other talmudic passages, including one in the tractate of *Yevamot* 49b in which Moses is described as having beheld God through a clear mirror, while the other prophets beheld Him in a dull glass. This thought is also present in the midrashic observation (*Leviticus Rabbah* 1) that all other prophets had to look into nine mirrors, whereas Moses glanced at only one a single time.

Another tendency in the Talmud is to give the Prophet Isaiah precedence over all other prophets—although it is stated that of the four nearly contemporary prophets, Isaiah, Amos, Micah, and Hosea, the last was first both in time and in importance (Talmud, *Pesachim* 87a). According to *Pirke de Rabbi Eliezer* (24:158a), Isaiah is responsible for more prophecies than any other prophet and he prophesied not only to Israel but to humankind as a whole. He received revelation directly from God and his prophecies were doubled (*Pirke de Rabbi Eliezer* 125b). Whereas the Prophet Ezekiel saw God as "a villager sees the person of the king," Isaiah was able to see God as "an inhabitant of a metropolis who sees the person of the king" (Talmud, *Chagiga* 13b). According to the Midrash (*Exodus Rabbah* 42), the words of all of the prophets were simply repetitions of Moses' words. In addition, with the exception of Moses and Isaiah, none of the prophets truly knew the content of their prophecies.

Another common stream of thought in talmudic times asserted that the prophets were not responsible for religious innovations or novel doctrines. Rather, their function was basically confined to explicating and illuminating the teachings of the Bible. According to the talmudic tractate of *Shabbat* 104a, the verse (Leviticus 27:34) "these are the commandments which God commanded Moses for the children of Israel in Mount Sinai" means that "henceforth a prophet may make no innovations." According to the Talmud (*Megillah* 14a), "the prophets neither took away nor added to anything that is written in the Torah," with the exception of the commandment to read the *Megillah*, and even for that they sought biblical sanction.

There are other rabbinic observations concerning the prophets and prophecy in general. The following are among the most noteworthy comments and assertions related to the subject of prophets and prophecy:

1. The number of prophets was innumerable ("double the number of the Israelite children that left Egypt") and every tribe produced them (Talmud, *Sukkah* 27b). However, only those persons' prophecies that bore a lesson for future generations were recorded. This amounted to the prophecies of forty-eight male prophets, seven female ones, and seven Gentile ones.

The sages did not list the forty-eight prophets by name. The following is a listing of them according to the great medieval biblical commentator Rashi (Talmud, *Megillah* 14a; *Halachot Gedolot*; and *Seder Olam*): Abraham; Isaac; Jacob; Moses, our teacher; Aaron; Joshua; Pinchas; Elkanah; Eli, the priest; Samuel of Ramah; Gad, the seer; Nathan, the prophet; King David; Ahijah, the Shilonite; King Solomon; Iddo, the seer; Shemaiah; Elijah, the prophet; Micaiah, son of Imlah; Obadiah; Hanani, the seer; Jehu, son of Hanani; Azariah, son of Oded; Ezekiel, the Levite, of the sons of Mattaniah; Eleazar, son of Dodavahu of Mareshah; Elisha, son of Shaphat; Jonah, son of Amittai; Hosea, son of Beeri; Amos; Amoz; Oded; Isaiah, son of Amoz; Micah of Moresheth; Joel, son of Pethuel; Nachum, the Elkoshite; Uriah, son of Shemaiah; Habbakuk; Zephaniah, son of Kushi; Jeremiah, son of Hilkiah; Ezekiel, son of Buzi the priest; Neriah; Baruch, son of Neriah; Seraiah; Mahseiah; Haggai; Zechariah; Malachi; and Mordecai.

The seven prophetesses included: Sarah, Miriam, Deborah, Hannah, Abigail, Huldah, and Esther.

The seven Gentile prophets included Balaam; his father, Beor (Talmud, *Sanhedrin* 105a); Job and his three companions; and Elisha, the son of Barachel (Talmud, *Bava Batra* 15b). Balaam was considered the greatest of all of the Gentile prophets. According to the Midrash (*Yalkut* 966 and *Numbers Rabbah* 14:34), Balaam was even regarded to be the equal of Moses. Nevertheless, Gentile prophecy was limited, in that prophecy came to them only by night and in "half words" and from "behind the curtain" (*Genesis Rabbah* 52:5).

2. All of the prophets only prophesied concerning Messianic times but were not permitted to see the heavenly world to come (Talmud, *Berachot* 34b).

3. The same message or sign was given to a number of prophets, but no two prophets prophesy in the same sign (Talmud, *Sanhedrin* 89a).

4. The use of anthropomorphism (i.e., the attribution of human characteristics to describe God) and metaphor by the prophets is regarded as a sign of their greatness (*Numbers Rabbah* 19:4).

5. With the exception of Jeremiah, all prophets begin with words of censure and conclude their prophecies on a note of hope of comfort (Jerusalem Talmud, *Berachot* 5:1, 8d).

6. Where the patronymic of the prophet is described, this is to assert that the prophet's father was also a prophet. When a prophet's place of origin is not mentioned, he is a Jerusalemite (Talmud, *Megillah* 15a).

7. All prophecies were included in the revelation at Mount Sinai (*Exodus Rabbah* 28).

8. The holy spirit did not descend upon each individual prophet to the same degree in each case. Some prophets received sufficient inspiration for one book, while others enough for two books, and others only so much as a couple of verses (*Leviticus Rabbah* 25).

9. Prophecy was often contingent upon the character of the generation among whom the potential prophet lived (Talmud, *Sanhedrin* 11a and *Berachot* 57a).

10. Only those prophecies were published that were valid for future days. Yet God will at some future time promulgate the many prophecies, which, because they deal only with the happenings of their

era, remain unpublished (*Song of Songs Rabbah* 4:11 and Talmud, *Megillah* 14a).

11. If made by a true and authentic prophet, the prediction of peace must come true. This does not hold true for a prediction of evil, for it is always possible that God may decide to withhold punishment (*Tanchuma Vayera* on 21:1).

12. A chaste bride is promised that prophets shall be among her sons (Talmud, *Megillah* 15a).

13. Isaiah is the greatest prophet, whereas Obadiah is the least great of all of the prophets (*Agadat Bereshit* 14).

14. The prophets' predictions of future blessings were intended to motivate Israel toward added piety (*Yalkut* 2:368 and *Ecclesiastes Rabbah* 1:8).

15. Eight prophets are said to have sprung from Rahab, the harlot (Talmud, *Megillah* 14a).

16. Fifty is the number given of the prophets among the returnees of the Babylon exile (*Zevachim* 62a).

17. Every tribe of Israel had a hand in producing prophets (Talmud, *Sukkah* 27a).

18. Since the destruction of the Temple in Jerusalem, prophecy has passed over to the wise, the fools, and the children, but the wise person is superior to the prophet (Talmud, *Bava Batra* 12a).

8

Notable Rabbinic Quotations on Prophecy

The following is a cross-section of rabbinic quotations and comments related to prophecy. Some of them are intended to elaborate upon the comments previously enumerated related to talmudic views of prophecy by providing the textual support for the comments.

1. Rabbi Pinchas ben Yair used to say: Torah leads to strictness, strictness to zeal, zeal to cleanliness, cleanliness to purity, purity to abstinence, abstinence to holiness, holiness to humility, humility to fear of sin, fear of sin to saintliness, saintliness to possession of the holy spirit, and the holy spirit to ability to revive the dead (Talmud, *Avodah Zarah* 20b and *Sotah* 9:9).

2. God's Presence rests only on one who is wise, strong, wealthy, tall in stature, yet unassuming (Talmud, *Shabbat* 92a and *Nedarim* 38a).

3. Rabbi Yochanan said: All of the prophets were rich. What is the proof? From Moses and Samuel, and from Amos and Jonah.

Moses, because he is quoted as saying, "I have not taken one ass from them" (Numbers 16:15), even as a fee. Perhaps it was because of his poverty? On the contrary, that Moses was wealthy is inferred from the verse "hew for yourself" (Exodus 34:1)—the chips of the broken tablets are to be yours (and will make you wealthy).

Samuel, because he is quoted as saying, "Here I am; witness against me before God and before His anointed; whose ox I have taken or whose ass have I taken?" (1 Samuel 12:2), even as a fee. But perhaps it was because of his poverty? On the contrary, that Samuel was wealthy is inferred from the verse "And his return was to Ramah" (1 Samuel 7:17), which Rava interpreted to mean that he had his household with him wherever he went.

Amos, because he is quoted as saying, "I am no prophet, neither am I a prophet's son, but I am the owner of herds, and a tender of sycamore figs" (Amos 7:14).

Jonah, because it is written, "He found a ship going to Tarshish and he paid the hire thereof" (Jonah 1:3). The hire of the whole ship, said Rabbi Yochanan, which, according to R. Romanus, came to four thousand gold denars (Talmud, *Nedarim* 38a).

4. Wherever the phrase "To David a Psalm" occurs, it denotes that God's Presence first rested on him and then he said that psalm. Whenever "A Psalm of David" occurs, it denotes that he first said

that psalm, and then the Divine Presence rested on him. This is to teach that God's Presence does not come to rest on a person in the midst of idleness or despair or laughter or levity or chitchat or idle talk, but only in the midst of joyous obedience to *mitzvot*. Thus, after Elisha grew angry at the King of Israel (2 Kings 3:13–14), his power of prophecy left him. But when he overcame anger, he found joy "in the playing of the instrument. It was only then that the hand of God and the power of prophecy returned to him" (2 Kings 3:15) (Talmud, *Pesachim* 117a and *Shabbat* 30b).

5. Rabbi Yudan said: Extremely wise in the power of language are the prophets, who speak of the form of the Almighty as though it were like the form of a man (*Genesis Rabbah* 27:1).

6. Rabbi Isaac ben Eleazar said: The prophets, knowing that their God was truthful, did not wish to flatter Him (Jerusalem Talmud, *Berachot* 7:4, 11c).

7. Rabbi Yose ben Zimra said: Just as a woman is not ashamed to demand the requirements of her household from her husband, so prophets are not ashamed to bluntly demand the requirements of Israel from the Holy One.

8. There are three types of prophets: One insisted on the honor due the Father (i.e., God), as well as the honor due the son (i.e., Israel); one insisted upon the honor due the Father without insisting upon the honor due the son; and one insisted upon

the honor due the son without insisting upon the honor due the Father. The Prophet Jeremiah insisted upon the honor due to the Father and the son, for he said, "We have sinned and rebelled; and You have not pardoned" (Lamentations 3:42). Therefore, his prophecy was doubled, as is said, "And there were added besides unto them many like words" (Jeremiah 36:32). Elijah insisted upon the honor due the Father but did not insist upon the honor due the son, as is said, "I have been very jealous for the Lord, the God of Hosts" (1 Kings 19:10). Consequently, what was he told? "Go, return on your way to the wilderness of Damascus . . . and Elisha the son of Shaphat . . . shall you anoint to succeed you as prophet" (1 Kings 19:15-16)— because I am displeased with your prophecy. Jonah insisted upon the honor due the son but did not insist upon the honor due the Father, as is said, "But Jonah arose up to flee from Tarshish from the presence of God" (Jonah 1:3). What is written about him? "The word of God came to Jonah a second time" (Jonah 3:1). God spoke to him a second time, but not a third.

Rabbi Jonathan said: Jonah embarked upon his voyage in order to drown himself in the sea, for the Bible says, "and he said unto them: 'Take me up and cast me forth into the sea'" (Jonah 1:12).

And so you find that the patriarchs as well as the prophets offered their lives on behalf of Israel. As to Moses, what is he quoted as saying? "And yet, if You would only forgive their sin! if not, blot me, I pray You, out of the book which You have written" (Exodus 32:32). And David, what did he say? "Lo, I have sinned, and I transgressed; but these sheep, what have they done? Let our hand, I pray You, be against me, and against my father's house" (2 Samuel 24:17). Thus, you see that everywhere patriarchs as well as prophets offered their lives for Israel (*Mechilta Bo, Pis'ha* 1).

9. "And God spoke to Moses that he say . . ." (Exodus 12:1). Rabbi Akiva taught: "That he say" means "Moses, go say to them that it was only because of their merit that God spoke with me." For during all the thirty-eight years in which God was angry with Israel, God did not speak with Moses, as is said, "So it came to pass, when all the men of war were consumed and dead from among the people, that God spoke to me, to say" (Deuteronomy 2:16–17). Rabbi Simeon ben Azzai stated: I am not arguing against the words of my teacher, but would merely add to what he taught: It was not with Moses alone that God spoke solely because of Israel's merit, but also with the other prophets—all of them—God spoke solely because of Israel's merit, as is said, "And I remained there appalled among them seven days" (Ezekiel 3:15). And after that it is written, "And it came to pass at the end of seven days, that the word of God came to me, to say" (Ezekiel 3:16). And similarly, "and it came to pass after ten days, that the word of God came again to Jeremiah" (Jeremiah 42:7).

In the account of Baruch, the son of Neriah, you will also find that he was complaining to God Who is everywhere, so that God had to tell Baruch, "You did say: Woe is me now, for God has added sorrow to my pain" (Jeremiah 45:3). You said, "Why was I treated differently from other disciples of the prophets? Joshua ministered to Moses, and the holy spirit rested upon him. Elisha ministered to Elijah, and the holy spirit rested upon him. Why then was I treated differently from other disciples of the prophets? 'I am weary with my groaning and I find no rest.'" The word "rest" here must mean "prophecy," as in the verse "and the spirit rested upon them and they prophesied in the camp" (Numbers 11:26) and in the verse "And the spirit of God shall rest upon him" (Isaiah 11:2). Note how God Who is everywhere told Jeremiah to answer Baruch: "Thus shall you say to him: 'Thus says God: Behold, that which I have built I am about to break down. And seek you great things for yourself?'" (Jeremiah 45:4–5). "Great things" here must mean "prophecy," as in the verse "Tell me, I pray you, all the great things that Elisha has done" (2 Kings 8:4) and in the verse "Call to Me, and I will answer you, and will tell you great things, and hidden, which you do not know" (Jeremiah 33:3). God went on, "Baruch, son of Neriah. If there is no vineyard, what need for a fence? If there is no flock, what need for a shepherd? Why should there be? 'Hence, when I bring evil upon all flesh, says God, in all places where you go, your life will be granted you (but not) prophecy'" (Jeremiah 45:5).

Thus, in each of the foregoing instances, you see that the prophets prophesy only because of Israel's merit (*Mechilta Bo, Pis'ha* 1).

10. Ulla said: Whenever a man's name is given along with that of his father as the author of prophecy, we know that he was a prophet as well as the son of a prophet. Where his own name is given

alone, without that of his father, we know that he was a prophet but not the son of a prophet. Where his name and the name of his hometown are stated, we know that he came from that town. Where his name is given but not the name of his town, we know that he was from Jerusalem (Talmud, *Megillah* 15a).

11. If a prophet's father's name is stated, we know that the father was also a prophet. But if a prophet's father's name is not stated, he was definitely not a prophet, except for Amos, whose father was a prophet even though his name is not stated. For the Bible says, "Amos answered Amaziah: 'I am not a prophet, and I am not a prophet's son'" (Amos 7:14). Even as Amos was a prophet, though he said, "I am not a prophet," so Amos's father was a prophet, though he said, "I am not a prophet's son."

If a prophet's home city is stated, we know he came from that city. If a prophet's city is not stated, we know he came from Jerusalem, for the majority of both prophets and sages came from Jerusalem, which the Bible describes as a city "full of justice, righteousness lodges in her" (Isaiah 1:21), implying that they who lodge in her are "sovereigns [prophets] of righteousness" (*Mishnat Rabbi Eliezer* 6).

12. Prophets were called by ten names: envoy (Obadiah 1:1), man of faith (Numbers 12:7), servant (Isaiah 49:5), messenger (Isaiah 6:8), visionary (Amos 7:12), sentinel (Ezekiel 3:17), seer (1 Samuel 9:9), angel (Haggai 1:13), prophet (Jeremiah 1:5), and man of God (Psalms 90:1).

The holy spirit is known by ten names: parable

(Micah 2:4), metaphor (Habbakuk 2:6), riddle (Ezekiel 17:2), speech (Jeremiah 5:13), speech (*Genesis Rabbah* 5:1), saying (*Sifre Leviticus* 3a), call (*Genesis Rabbah* 20:2), command (Isaiah 17:1:2), pronouncement (2 Chronicles 15:8), prophecy (Joel 3:1), and vision (*Genesis Rabbah* 44:6).

13. Prophecy is known by ten names, six gentle and four stern: prophecy, seeing, watching, parable, metaphor, and holy spirit are gentle; vision, pronouncement, preaching, and riddle are stern.

God spoke with the patriarchs through seeing, prophecy, and vision. With Moses our teacher, through prophecy, seeing, and the holy spirit. With the other prophets, God communicated through most or some of these means.

Prophetic speech is to be understood as relevant to the immediate need as well as beyond the immediate need, as in the verse "Walk before Me, and be perfect" (Genesis 17:1) and in "Let it not be grievous in your sight because of the lad" (Genesis 21:12). On the other hand, speech that is not prophetic is to be understood as bearing only on the immediate need, as in the verse "Behold, you shall die, because of the woman" (Genesis 20:3) and in "Take heed to yourself that you speak not to Jacob either good or bad" (Genesis 31:29).

When a dream is not prophetic—he who had it has to ask for its interpretation, as with Pharaoh's dream (Genesis 41), Nebuchadnezzar's dream (Daniel 2), and the Midianite's dream (Judges 7:13). But when a dream *is* prophetic, even if its matter is enigmatic—he who had it need not ask for its interpretation, as with Daniel and his companions.

As for the patriarchs, when the Holy One appeared to them in order to speak to them, He did not reveal Himself through the celestial creatures, through the chariot, or through other aspects of God's glory. For God's Presence rested directly upon the patriarchs.

Rabbi Simeon said: The patriarchs themselves are the chariot, for it is said of Jacob, "And God Himself went up from him" (Genesis 35:13). But as for the other prophets, God revealed Himself to each of them through aspects of His glory, in keeping with each one's capacity (*Mishnat Rabbi Eliezer* 6).

14. "He makes weight for the spirit" (Job 28:25). Rabbi Acha said: Even the holy spirit, which rests on the prophets, does so by specific weight—one prophet uttering one book of prophecy, and another two. Rabbi Simon said: Beeri uttered two verses as a prophet, and because there was not enough to make a book, they were included in the Book of Isaiah. The two verses are "And when they shall say unto you: 'Seek unto the ghosts and the familiar spirits'" (Isaiah 8:19) and its companion verse.

"He makes weight for the spirit." Each and every prophet had the holy spirit set aside within him, each according to his capacity (*Leviticus Rabbah* 15:2).

15. Rabbi Isaac said: "Several prophets treated the same theme, yet no two prophets prophesied on that theme in the same language" (Talmud, *Sanhedrin* 89a).

16. "When I spoke to the prophets, I multiplied visions" (Hosea 12:11). The Holy One said: It is true that "I spoke to the prophets," but "I multiplied visions," for among all of them, the experience in prophecy of one is not like the experience in prophecy in another. Amos saw Me standing (Amos 9:1). Micaiah saw Me seated (2 Chronicles 18:18). Moses saw Me as a mighty man (Exodus 15:3). Daniel saw Me as an ancient of days. Therefore, it is written, "By the ministry of the prophets have I used similitudes (Daniel 7) (*Aggadat Bereshit* 14 (ed. Buber [Cracow, 1902], p. 30).

17. Some, such as the Prophet Ezekiel, prophesied through seeing: "I saw visions of God" (Ezekiel 1:1); Habbakuk, through hearing: "I have heard that which You have made heard" (Habbakuk 3:2); Jeremiah, through the mouth: "God touched my mouth . . . 'Behold, I have put My words in your mouth'" (Jeremiah 1:9). Some, through the nose: "And spirit entered into me" (Ezekiel 2:2). Some, through the hand: "By the hand of the prophets have I used similitudes" (Hosea 12:11). Some prophesied in enigmas, and some in enigmas within enigmas (*Yalkut Chadash* [Warsaw, 1879], Noah).

18. Rabbi Eleazar taught, in the name of Rabbi Yose ben Zimra: As they uttered their prophecies, none of the prophets knew what they were prophesying, except Moses and Joshua, who did know. Rabbi Joshua bar Nehemiah maintained that Elijah also prophesied and knew what he was prophesying.

Rabbi Eleazar further taught, in the name of

Rabbi Yose ben Zimra: Samuel, the master of prophets, did not know what he was prophesying while uttering his prophecy, as is said, "And the Lord sent Jerubbaal, and Bedan, and Jephtha, and Samuel" (1 Samuel 12:11). Samuel did not say, "God sent . . . me," but "God sent . . . Samuel, "for he did not know what he was prophesying (*Mechilta Tehillim* 90:4; *Yalkut Psalm* 841).

19. "And there has not arisen a prophet in Israel since like unto Moses" (Deuteronomy 34:10). What is the difference between Moses and all the other prophets? Rabbi Judah, son of Rabbi Ilai, and the sages differed in their explanations. Rabbi Judah said: The prophets beheld prophetic visions through nine lenses. This is intimated in the verse "And the appearance of the vision which I saw was like the vision that I saw when I came to destroy the city; and the visions were like the vision that I saw by the river Chebar, and I fell upon my face" (Ezekiel 43:3)—thus, nine visions.

Likewise, it is said of Daniel, "And he gave heed to the word, and had understanding of the vision . . . I lifted up mine eyes and saw . . . his face as the appearance of lightning . . . And I, Daniel, alone saw the vision; for the men that were with me saw not the vision . . . so I was left alone, and saw this great vision" (Daniel 10:1 and 10:5–8)—thus, again nine visions. But Moses our teacher saw through only one lens, as is said, "With him do I speak in one vision, and not in riddles" (Numbers 12:8).

However, the sages said: all other prophets saw their visions through a blurred lens, as is said, "I have multiplied visions; and by the ministry of the prophets have I used similitudes" (Hosea 12:11). But Moses saw his vision through a polished lens, as is said, "The similitude of God does he behold" (Numbers 12:8). All the other prophets heard the voice only in keeping with their capacity, as is said, "The voice of God, according to a man's capacity" (Psalms 29:4). But Moses our teacher heard it in full, as is said, "And he heard the voice" (Numbers 7:89)—the voice as it is (*Leviticus Rabbah* 1:14).

20. Rabbi Jonah said, in the name of Rabbi Samuel bar Nachman: Every prophet that arose repeated the prophecy of his predecessor. Why did he do this? To make the predecessor's prophecy quite clear.

But Rabbi Joshua ben Levi said: Every prophet was fully engaged with his own prophecy, except for Moses, who uttered all of the prophecies of the other prophets as well as his own, with the result that whoever prophesied later drew from the prophecy of Moses (*Exodus Rabbah* 42:8).

21. Rabbi Yose bar Hanina said: Our teacher Moses pronounced four adverse decrees against Israel, but four subsequent prophets came and rescinded them. Moses said: "Israel dwells in safety, alone, in Jacob's abode" (Deuteronomy 33:28). But Amos came and revoked it when he prayed to God, "Refrain. How will Jacob survive alone? He is so small" (Amos 7:5). We are told in the next verse, "God relented concerning this" (Amos 7:6). Moses said, "Among those nations you shall find no peace" (Deuteronomy 28:65). But Jeremiah came and said, "The people that were left of the sword, Israel, I go

to give him peace" (Jeremiah 31:1). Moses said, "Visiting the iniquity of the fathers upon the children" (Exodus 34:7). But Ezekiel came and nullified it: "The soul that sins, it shall die" (Ezekiel 18:20). Moses said, "You shall be lost among the nations" (Leviticus 26:38). But Isaiah came and said, "It shall come to pass on that day, that a great horn shall be blown, and they shall come that were lost" (Isaiah 27:13) (Talmud, *Makkot* 24a).

22. Rabbi Simon said: The face of Pinchas, when the holy spirit rested on him, glowed like torches (*Leviticus Rabbah* 1:1).

23. "The spirit of God began to ring within him" (Judges 13:25). Rabbi Nachman said: "Samson, when the spirit of God rested upon him, the hairs on his head stood up and clanged against one another as in a bell" (*Leviticus Rabbah* 8:2).

24. "He wakens me morning by morning. He wakens my ear to hear what a disciple should hear" (Isaiah 50:4). Isaiah said: As I walked about in my house of study, "I heard the voice of God, saying: 'Whom shall I send, and who will go for us?' (Isaiah 6:8) When I sent Micaiah (1 Kings 22:24), they smote him on the cheek. When I sent Amos, they mockingly called him 'tongue-heavy.' Now 'whom shall I send, and who will go for us?' "

Isaiah replied, "Here I am, send me" (Isaiah 6:8). The Holy One warned him: "Isaiah, My children are obstinate, troublesome. If you are willing to suffer insults and be smitten by them, you may go on My mission, but if not, you may not go." Isaiah replied, "Even if such be my portion, 'I am ready to give my body to the smiters, and my cheek to them that pluck off the hair' (Isaiah 50:6). But I am unworthy of going to Your children on a mission of Yours." The Holy One answered, "Isaiah, 'you have loved righteousness' (Psalms 45:8), you have loved to make out My children to be righteous; 'and hate wickedness,' hated to make them out wicked. 'Therefore I, God, your God, have Myself anointed you with the oil of gladness of your fellows.'" What is meant by "above your fellows?" In using these words, the Holy One meant: As you live, each of the prophets who prophesied before you received his prophetic mission from another prophet. As the Bible relates, the spirit of Moses rested on the seventy elders. "God took of the spirit that was on him, and put it upon the seventy elders" (Numbers 11:25). "The spirit of Elijah rested on Elisha" (2 Kings 2:15). But you alone will prophesy directly from the mouth of the Divine Power, so that you can say, "The spirit of the Lord God is upon me, because God has anointed me" (Isaiah 61:1). More. By your life, all the other prophets who prophesied used single terms in their prophecies. But you will prophesy in double terms (revealing that you prophesy with a double portion of the Divine Power). "Awake, awake" (Isaiah 51:9). "Rouse yourself, rouse yourself" (Isaiah 51:17); "Rejoicing, I will rejoice" (Isaiah 61:10). "I, even I, am He that comforts you" (Isaiah 51:12). Comfort you, comfort you, my people" (Isaiah 40:1) (*Leviticus Rabbah* 10:2).

25. Rava said: All that Ezekiel saw, Isaiah saw. Whom does Ezekiel resemble? A villager who

saw the king. Whom does Isaiah resemble? A city dweller who saw the king [i.e., and therefore, the king appeared to the city dweller as a familiar sight] (Rashi, Talmud, *Chagigah* 13b).

26. "Before I formed you in the belly, I knew you" (Jeremiah 1:5). That is, even before I formed you in the belly of your mother, I designated you to prophesy to My people. In answer, Jeremiah spoke right up to the Holy One: Master of the Universe, I cannot prophesy to them. What prophet ever came before them whom they did not seek to slay? When You set up Moses and Aaron over them to act in their behalf, did they not wish to stone them? When You set up the curly-haired Elijah over them to act in their behalf, they mocked and ridiculed him, saying, "Look how he frizzes his locks, this fancy haired fellow." And when you set up Elisha over them to act in their behalf, they said derisively to him, "Go away, baldhead, go away, baldhead" (2 Kings 2:23). Besides, I cannot venture forth in Israel's behalf, because "I do not know how to speak, for I am still a child" (Jeremiah 1:6). The divine spirit replied, "Is it not because you are a child that I love you?" For Jeremiah had not as yet tasted the savor of transgression (*Pesikta Rabbati* 26:1).

27. Jeremiah was one of three prophets who prophesied in that generation—Jeremiah, Zephaniah, and the prophetess Hulda. Jeremiah prophesied in the city squares, Zephaniah in the Temple and in synagogues, and Huldah among the women (*Pesikta Rabbati* 1).

28. Although all the prophets begin their books with recitals of Israel's guilt, they end them with words of comfort (Jerusalem Talmud, *Berachot* 5:1, 8d).

29. "And this is the blessing" (Deuteronomy 33:1). Because at the beginning Moses spoke harsh words to Israel, he then changed and spoke words of comfort to them. And the other prophets learned from him, for at the beginning they spoke harsh words to Israel, but then they changed and spoke words of comfort to them" (*Sifra Deuteronomy* 342).

30. "And there has not arisen a prophet since in Israel" (Deuteronomy 34:10). There had not arisen one like him in Israel; but among the nations of the world, one like him did arise. This was done in order that the nations of the world might have no excuse to say, "If we had a prophet like Moses, we would have worshiped the Holy One." Who was the prophet like Moses they had? Balaam, son of Beor. However, there was a difference between the prophecy of Moses and the prophecy of Balaam, in that Moses had three qualities Balaam did not have: when God spoke with Moses, Moses was able to stand on his feet, whereas when God spoke with Balaam, he fell prone on the ground. He spoke with Moses mouth to mouth, whereas God did not speak mouth to mouth with Balaam. God spoke with Moses in plain terms, whereas God spoke with Balaam only in parables. On the other hand, there were three qualities Balaam had that Moses did not have: Moses did not know who was speaking to him, whereas Balaam knew who was speaking to him;

Moses did not know when the Holy One would speak to him, whereas Balaam knew when the Holy One would speak to him (Balaam's knowledge in these two respects may be explained by the parable of a king's cook, who knew what fare the king would have on his table and how much money would be spent by the king for this purpose); Moses could not speak with God whenever he wished, whereas Balaam spoke with God whenever he pleased, as the Bible says, "Fallen down—his eyes are opened" (Numbers 24:4), which implies that whenever he prostrated himself on his face, at once his eyes were opened (*Numbers Rabbah* 14:20).

31. The Holy One raised up Moses for Israel and raised up Balaam for the nations of the world. Observe the difference between the prophets of Israel and the prophets of the nations of the world. The prophets of Israel warn Israel against three transgressions. Thus Ezekiel: "I have appointed you a watchman unto the House of Israel . . . and you shall give them warning" (Ezekiel 3:17). But the one prophet who rose up among the nations made a breach in the moral order through his desire to cause human beings to perish from the world. More! All the prophets had a measure of compassion for Israel as well as for the nations of the world. Thus, Isaiah said, "Wherefore my heart moans for Moab like a harp" (Isaiah 16:11). Likewise, Ezekiel said, "Take up a lamentation for Tyre" (Ezekiel 27:2). But this one, a cruel man, rose up to root out an entire people for no fault whatsoever (*Tanchuma* B) (ed. Solomon Buber, Vilna 1885).

32. Rabbi Isaac said: Until the Tabernacle was erected, prophecy was also found among the nations of the world; after the Tabernacle was set up, it departed from among them, as Israel, said, "I beheld the holy spirit and will not let it go" (Song of Songs 3:4). The sages retorted to Rabbi Isaac: But Balaam did prophesy after the Tabernacle was erected. He replied: Yes, but he prophesied for the good of Israel. For example, 'Who counts the dust of Jacob? (Numbers 2:10); "None has beheld iniquity in Jacob" (Numbers 23:21); "There is no augury in Jacob" (Numbers 23:23); "How goodly are your tents, O Jacob" (Numbers 24:5); "There shall step forth a star out of Jacob" (Numbers 24:17); and "Out of Jacob shall one have dominion" (Numbers 24:19) (*Leviticus Rabbah* 1:12).

33. Seven prophets prophesied to the peoples of the world: Balaam and his father; Job; Eliphaz, the Temanite; Bildad, the Shuhite; Zophar, the Naamathite; and Elihu, the son of Barachel, the Buzite (Talmud, *Bava Batra* 15b).

34. What is the difference between the prophets of Israel and the prophets of the nations of the world? Rabbi Hama, the son of Rabbi Hanina, said: To the prophets of the nations of the world, the Holy One appears with half-speech only. But to the prophets of Israel, with complete speech, clear speech, affectionate speech, in the language of purity, in the language of holiness, in the same language in which the ministering angels chant praise to God.

Rabbi Yose said: The Holy One appears to the prophets of the nations of the world only at night when human beings generally take leave from one another, as Elophas said: "A word was secretly brought to me . . . at the time of leave-taking, from the visions of the night, when deep sleep falls on men" (Job 4:12–13).

Rabbi Hanina bar Papa said: The matter may be illustrated by the parable of a king placed with his friend in a chamber where a curtain was between them. Whenever the king wished to speak to his friend, he would raise the curtain by folding it upward until he saw his friend face-to-face and then speak to him. But for the nations of the world, God does not fold up the curtain. God speaks to them from behind the curtain.

Rabbi Simon said: The matter may be illustrated by the parable of a king who has a wife and a concubine. To his wife he goes openly, but to his concubine he goes secretly. So, too, the Holy One reveals Himself to the nations of the world only at night, but to the prophets of Israel by day (*Genesis Rabbah* 52:5).

35. The prophets of Israel do not know when the Holy One will speak to them, but the prophets of the nations of the world do know when the Holy One will speak to them. Thus, it is said of Balaam, "The saying of him who knows when he is about to hear the words of God" (Numbers 24:4). The prophets of Israel do not know how many utterances God will articulate for them. But the prophets of the nations of the world do know how many utterances God will articulate for them. Thus, it is said of Balaam, "Who knows the knowledge of the Most High" (Numbers 24:16).

Are the prophets of the nations of the world then greater than the prophets of Israel? Not at all. In fact, the prophets of Israel are greater than the prophets of the nations of the world. A parable will explain the matter. The king's cooks know in advance exactly what expenditures they have to make, what ingredients they will have to prepare, because their charge has definite limits. But the king's governors do not know in advance what expenditures they have to make and what items they have to prepare, because their charge has no definite limit.

Rabbi Issachar said: With the prophets of the nations of the world, God speaks only in half-speech. Thus, the Bible says, "God called [*vayikkar*, without the letter *alef* at the end] unto Balaam" (Numbers 23:4). But with the prophets of Israel, God speaks in full speech, as, for example, "God called [*vayikra*, with the letter *alef* at the end] unto Moses" (Exodus 19:20), a mode of locution the ministering angels use to praise Him, as is said, "And one called [*kara*] unto another, and said" (Isaiah 6:6) (*Mishnat Rabbi Eliezer* 6).

36. Rabbi Levi said: The prophecy of the nations of the world is ambiguous, so that they do not know whether they are told to slay or told to be slain. A parable of one who, while on a journey, grew tired toward evening. So he said: O, that I had just one ass. A Roman, whose she-ass had just then foaled, passed by and said to him: Take this newborn foal and carry it on your back. So he said: I see that my prayer has been answered, but I did not put it

properly—whether to ride, or be ridden (*Midrash, Panim Acharim A*, pp. 50–51).

37. The Holy One said to the prophets: What do you suppose—if you refuse to go on a mission of Mine, I have no other messenger? "With the superfluities of the earth, with all" (Ecclesiastes 5:8)—I can have My mission carried out with all, even by means of a serpent, even by means of a scorpion, even by means of a frog (*Exodus Rabbah* 10:1).

38. Before the Land of Israel had been chosen, all lands were suitable for Divine revelations; after the Land of Israel had been chosen, all other lands were eliminated. Before the Temple had been singled out, all of Jerusalem was suitable for the abiding of the Presence; after the Temple had been singled out, the rest of Jerusalem was eliminated.

You might say, "I can cite instances of prophets with whom God spoke outside the Land." True, God did speak to them outside the Land, but only because of the merit of the fathers did He speak to them. And even though, because of the merits of the fathers, He did speak with them outside of the Land, God spoke with them only at a spot that was pure, being near water, as Daniel said, "I was by the stream Ulai" (Daniel 8:2); and again, "I was by the side of the great river, which is the Tigris" (Daniel 10:4); and elsewhere, the Bible says, "The word of God came expressly to Ezekiel the Priest the son of Buzi by the river Chebar" (Ezekiel 1:3).

Rabbi Eleazar ben Zadok added: Note that the Bible says, "Arise, go forth into the plain" (Ezekiel

3:22), asserting that a plain was suitable for Divine revelation.

You can see for yourself that God's Presence does not reveal itself outside the Land. The Bible says, "But Jonah rose up to flee from Tarshish from the Presence of God" (Jonah 1:3). Could he really have thought that it was possible to flee from God? Had it not already been said, "Whither shall I go from Your spirit? Or whither shall I flee from Your Presence?" (Psalms 139:7)? But Jonah thought: In order not to incriminate the Jews, for Gentiles are more prone to repent, I will go outside the Land, where the Presence does not reveal itself. A parable will illustrate his foolishness. A priest's servant who fled from his master said: I will go to the cemetery, a place where my master cannot follow me. His master told him, "I have other flunkeys just like you." So, too, when Jonah said, "I will go outside the Land to a place where the Presence does not reveal itself," the Holy One replied, "I have other emissaries like you, as is said, 'God hurled a great wind into the sea'" (Jonah 1:4) (*Mechilta Bo, Pis'ha* 1).

39. When Rabbi Huna died, Rabbi Abba began his eulogy by saying: Our master was worthy of having the Presence rest on him, but his residing in Babylonia prevented it (Talmud, *Moed Katan* 25a).

40. Many prophets rose up for Israel, twice as many as the number of Israelites who went out of Egypt. But only prophecy required by subsequent generations was set down in writing, while proph-

ecy not required by subsequent generations was not set down (Talmud, *Megillah* 14a).

41. Rabbi Derosa said, in the name of Rabbi Samuel bar Isaac: Sixty myriads of prophets rose up for Israel in the days of Elijah. Why was their prophecy not made public? Because it was not required for subsequent generations. Hence you may conclude that any prophecy that had meaning for the time and was also required for subsequent generations was made public, while any prophecy that had meaning for the time but was not required for subsequent generations was not made public. In the time to come, however, the Holy One will bring these prophets back and make public their prophecies, as is said, "The Lord my God shall come, and all the holy ones with you" (Zechariah 14:5).

Rabbi Berekhiah said, in the name of Rabbi Helbo: Even as sixty myriads of prophets rose up for Israel, so sixty myriads of prophetesses rose up for them, and Solomon came along and made the fact public when he said, "Your lips also, O My bride, drop honey" (Song of Songs 4:11) (*Song of Songs Rabbah* 4:11).

42. Our masters taught: After the early prophets died, the *Urim* and *Tummim* ceased (Talmud, *Sotah* 9:12).

43. After the last prophets—Haggai, Zechariah, and Malachi—died, the holy spirit departed from Israel, which nevertheless were able to avail themselves of the Divine voice (Talmud, *Sanhedrin* 11a).

44. Rabbi Avdimi of Haifa said: Ever since the Temple was destroyed, prophecy was taken from the prophets and given to the sages.

Rabbi Yochanan said: Ever since the Temple was destroyed, prophecy was taken from the prophets and given to fools and children (Talmud, *Bava Batra* 12a–b).

45. The dream is an unripe form of prophecy (*Genesis Rabbah* 17:5).

46. Rabbi Yochanan said: When a man rises early and a verse comes to his mouth, it is a kind of minor prophecy (Talmud, *Berachot* 55b).

47. Rabbi Judah said, in the name of Rav: Whoever is boastful, if he is a sage, his wisdom leaves him. If he is a prophet, his prophecy departs from him.

Resh Lakish said: Whoever is prone to anger, if he is a sage, his wisdom departs from him; if he is a prophet, his prophecy departs from him.

48. "These are the commandments" (Leviticus 27:34) implies that henceforth no prophet may introduce innovations (Talmud, *Shabbat* 104a).

49. Our masters taught: Forty-eight prophets and seven prophetesses prophesied to Israel, but they neither diminished from nor added to anything that is written in the Torah, other than the reading of the *Megillah*.

How did they who introduced the *Megillah* reading infer it from the Torah? Rabbi Chiyya bar Avin said, in the name of Rabbi Joshua ben Korcha: If we hymn praise for being delivered from slavery into freedom, should we not do so all the more for being delivered from death to life? (Talmud, *Megillah* 14a).

50. The false prophet who prophesies what he has not heard or what he has not been told—his death shall be at the hands of man. But he who suppresses his prophecy (e.g., Jonah) or disregards the words of another prophet or the prophet who transgresses his own words—his death shall be at the hands of heaven.

One who prophesies in the name of an alien god and says, "Thus says the alien god," is liable to death by strangling, even if he follows the *halachah* in declaring unclean what is unclean and clean what is clean (Talmud, *Sanhedrin* 11:6).

51. Rabbi Abbahu said, in the name of Rabbi Yochanan: In every matter, if a prophet tells you, "Violate the commandments of Torah," listen to him, except in the matter of idolatry: then, even if the prophet should cause the sun to stand still in midheaven, do not listen to him.

Rabbi Akiva said: Far be it from the Holy One to have the sun stand still at the behest of those who transgress His will. But the Torah refers here to such as Hananiah, son of Azur, who at first was a true prophet and only subsequently a false prophet (Talmud, *Sanhedrin* 90a).

52. One who shouts loudly during the *Tefillah* is among the false prophets (Talmud, *Berachot* 24b).

9

Lessons Derived from the Rabbinic Quotations

The following conclusions and lessons regarding prophecy can be derived from the previously enumerated talmudic and rabbinic quotations:

1. Characteristics of a prophet include learning Torah, avoiding sin, cleanliness, purity, holiness, humility, fear of sin, and saintliness.

2. God's Presence rests only on persons who are wise and strong, yet unassuming.

3. Prophets are very strong when it comes to the usage of language and speech.

4. Prophets are never ashamed to bluntly demand the requirements of Israel from God.

5. When a man's name is given along with that of his father as the author of the prophecy, that man is a prophet as well as the son of a prophet. Where

his own name is given alone without that of his father, we know that he was a prophet but not the son of a prophet.

6. Where a prophet's name and the name of his hometown is stated, the prophet came from that town. Where the name is given but not the town's name, the prophet is from Jerusalem.

7. Prophets had many names, including: envoy, man of faith, servant, messenger, visionary, sentinel, seer, angel, prophet, and man of God.

8. God's Holy Spirit is known by many names, including parable, metaphor, riddle, speech, saying, call, command, pronouncement, prophecy, and vision.

9. No two prophets prophesied on the same theme in identical language.

10. God appeared to prophets in a variety of visions.

11. Moses was a prophet superior to the others, able to see his visions through a polished lens.

12. Every prophet who arose repeated the prophecy of his predecessor.

13. Some prophets (e.g., Jeremiah) were predestined to be prophets even before being born.

14. All prophets begin their books with recitals of Israel's guilt and conclude them on a note of comfort and hope.

15. After the Tabernacle was erected, prophecy left the nations of the world.

16. Before the Land of Israel had been chosen, all lands were suitable for Divine revelations. After the Land of Israel had been chosen, all other lands were eliminated.

17. Prophets to nations of the world appeared with half-speech, while prophets of Israel appeared with complete speech.

18. After the last prophet died (i.e., Malachi), prophecy ceased to exist.

19. Dreams are a form of prophecy in an unripened state.

20. Prophets neither diminished nor added to what was written in the Torah, with the exception of the reading of the *Megillah* on Purim.

10

The Rabbis' List of Prophets

In the Bible we are never told how many prophets there were or, in some instances, who delivered certain prophecies. However, the rabbis of old preserved some relevant information. The sages stated that forty-eight prophets and seven prophetesses arose in Israel, but they did not list them by name. The question, therefore, is from which period one should begin to enumerate these prophets. Different schools of thought have come forward with different answers. Rashi, the medieval Bible commentator, in agreement with *Seder Olam*, identifies Abraham as the first prophet. Rabbenu Hananel, and later the Gaon of Vilna, identifies Moses as the first prophet. Furthermore, while Rashi lists forty-eight prophets and seven prophetesses (Talmud, *Megillah* 14a), according to the Vilna Gaon there are five lists in all, these being:

1. Seven Hebrew prophets prior to Israel's descent into Egypt
2. Seven Hebrew prophets in Egypt

63

3. Seven heathen prophets
4. Forty-eight prophets who arose after the conquest of Canaan
5. Seven prophetesses

Here is a listing of the forty-eight prophets and seven prophetesses, according to Rashi, and a brief summary of each, as cited in *The Graphic History of the Jewish Heritage*, edited by Pinchus Wollman Tsamir.

1. **Abraham:** He was the father of the Israelite nation and the first person to advance the monotheistic concept of one God. According to one rabbinic tradition, Abraham acknowledged God's existence when he was but three years old (Talmud, *Nedarim* 32). According to *Genesis Rabbah* 43, he converted scores of people to monotheism. The land of Canaan was promised to Abraham and his descendants. He left his homeland of Mespotamia at God's command and settled in Canaan. There he demonstrated his faith by offering up his beloved son Isaac for sacrifice. He fought with local Canaanite kings to rescue his nephew Lot and he pleaded with God to spare the wicked city of Sodom for the sake of a few righteous inhabitants.

2. **Isaac:** Second of the three patriarchs, he was the only son of Abraham by his wife Sarah. Saved from the ordeal of child sacrifice, Isaac symbolized man's devotion to God. Blind in his old age, he is deceived by his wife, Rebekah, and his son Jacob, but seems helpless to undo the wrong done to the firstborn Esau, cheated of the paternal blessing.

The sounding of the ram's horn on the Jewish New Year of Rosh Hashanah is considered to be a reminder of the sacrificial binding of Isaac: "Sound the ram's horn, so that I may be reminded of the binding of Isaac, the son of Abraham" (Talmud, *Rosh Hashanah* 16).

3. **Jacob:** Third of the patriarchs, Jacob was the father of the twelve tribes of Israel. He suffered greatly in his lifetime from his brother Esau's enmity, from the machinations of his uncle Laban, from the death of his wife Rachel, and from the sale of his beloved son Joseph. Twice angels appeared to him, the last time when he was returning from Haran. Therefore, he wrestled with the angel of God and prevailed. With this victory, he gained the name of "Israel."

4. **Moses:** Moses was the spiritual architect of the Jewish people. Considered by the rabbis to be the greatest of all the prophets, the Book of Deuteronomy 34:10 asserts that "there has not arisen a prophet like unto Moses, who God knew face to face." Moses helped to deliver the children of Israel from Egyptian bondage, leading them for forty years in the wilderness. There, he received the Ten Commandments atop of Mount Sinai.

The sages declared that Moses was equal to all six hundred thousand Israelites (*Song of Songs Rabbah* 1).

5. **Aaron:** Older brother of Moses, Aaron was a spokesman before Pharaoh. He substituted for Moses when the latter ascended to Mount Sinai to

receive the Ten Commandments. The people turned to Aaron when they wished to make a golden calf (Exodus 32:1). According to the sages, Aaron bowed to the will of the people because he sought to prevent bloodshed (Talmud, *Sanhedrin* 7). After the Tabernacle was built, Aaron and his descendants were chosen for the priesthood.

The rabbis declared that the "cloud of glory" accompanied the Israelites throughout their wandering in the desert because of Aaron's presence and that when he died, the clouds departed (Talmud, *Taanit* 9).

6. **Joshua:** Joshua was chosen by Moses to succeed him as leader of the Israelites. He led the new generation of Israel into Canaan and conquered the land, dividing it among the twelve tribes. A fearless warrior, he led the Israelites in battle in the desert and defeated Amalek in Rephidim.

The rabbis noted that Joshua judged the people for fourteen years (*Seder Olam*). Ten ordinances for civil welfare are attributed to him (Talmud, *Bava Kamma* 80b) as well as the composition of some of the psalms of *Hallel* (Talmud, *Pesachim* 117).

7. **Pinchas:** According to Maimonides in his introduction to the *Mishneh Torah*, Pinchas received the Torah directly from Moses. Pinchas was the High Priest in the time of Moses, the son of Eleazar and the grandson of Aaron. When the children of Israel under Moses stopped at Shittim, they began to dally with the gods of Moab and with Moabite women. This angered God, Who threatened to destroy the Israelites, sending a plague. Moses or-

dered the judges among his people to sentence to death any person bowing down to Baal of Peor, the Moabite god. At that moment an Israelite came into the camp with a Midianite woman. Pinchas was so incensed that he "took a spear in his hand and went after the man of Israel into the inner room, and pierced both of them . . . (Numbers 25:8). The plague was stopped, but not before twenty-four thousand of them had died.

8. **Elkanah:** According to rabbinic tradition, Elkanah was one of the major prophets, "unparalleled in his generation" (*Megillah* 14, Numbers 10:12). A descendant of the tribe of Levi, who dwelt in Mount Ephraim, he was deemed worthy of fathering a great son by his pious wife Hannah—namely, Samuel.

According to rabbinic lore, Elkanah is referred to in the verse that reads: "There came a man of God unto Eli" (1 Samuel 2:27), for he is one of ten persons known as "the man of God" (*Yalkut Shimoni*, 1 Samuel, para. 93).

9. **Eli, the Priest:** Both priest and prophet, Eli was one of the sons of Itamar, son of Aaron. He was the last High Priest to officiate in Shiloh. Eli died at the age of ninety-eight, upon hearing that the Ark of God had been captured by the Philistines. According to Maimonides, he received the tradition from the elders and from Pinchas.

10. **Samuel:** Samuel was the son of Elkanah and the last judge of Israel. As a child he served in the Temple at Shiloh, where he had been brought by

his mother. There the prophetic spirit came upon him and he foresaw that the house of Eli would be destroyed because of the sins of the priest's sons (1 Samuel 3). When Samuel reached manhood he attained fame as a prophet throughout the land. He renewed prophecy in Israel. As a young man, seeing that visions were infrequent among the people (1 Samuel 3:1), he established schools for prophecy in Ramah (1 Samuel 19:18–24).

11. **David, son of Jesse:** The sages include David among the prophets on the basis of the many psalms and prayers ascribed to him. According to Maimonides, David received the tradition from Samuel and his court.

12. **Gad, the Seer:** The Bible refers to Gad as both prophet and seer (1 Chronicles 29:29). He accompanied and advised David during the latter's wanderings (1 Samuel 22:5). According to the sages, Gad was one of the authors of the chronicles of Samuel and also helped David organize the Levitical singers in the Temple (1 Chronicles 23:27; Talmud, *Taanit* 15).

13. **Nathan, the Prophet:** Nathan was considered the most outstanding prophet in the generation that followed Samuel. He admonished David fearlessly for the latter's misconduct with Bathsheba (2 Samuel 12). On the other hand, he predicted that the house of David would have perpetual dominion over Israel and that Jerusalem would be a holy city (2 Samuel 7:16; 1 Chronicles 28:4). This prophecy had a great effect upon Jewish religious thought

and on the teachings of other religions deriving from Judaism.

14. Ahijah, the Shilonite: When Solomon sinned, Ahijah prophesied the division of the kingdom and instigated Jeroboam to take the seceding ten tribes. When his hopes for Jeroboam were not realized, he prophesied the fall of Jeroboam's dynasty.

Rabbinic legend relates that Ahijah was a Levite who was born during the days of Amram, father of Moses, and who died during the lifetime of Elijah, whose teacher he was (Talmud, *Bava Batra* 121). Rabbi Simeon, son of Yochai, praised the prophet in this way: "If Abraham will agree to suffer for the sins of all the generations up to my time, I shall suffer for all generations up to the Messianic era. If he will not agree to this, then let Ahijah the Shilonite join me and together we shall carry the burden of sin from Abraham's time to the days of King Messiah" (*Genesis Rabbah* 35).

15. Solomon: The sages included Solomon among the prophets because of his dream at Gibeon wherein God appeared to him and said: "Ask what I shall give thee" and Solomon requested "an understanding heart" with which to judge the people (1 Kings 3:5,9). King Solomon was the builder of the Temple in Jerusalem and effected the golden age of the Israelite kingdom.

16. Iddo, the Seer: He preached during the reign of Jeroboam, son of Nebat, according to the rabbis. It was he who came from Judah to Beth El and prophesied the destruction of the altar that Jeroboam had built there and had sacrificed upon (1 Kings 13:2).

17. Shemaiah, the Man of God: A Judean, Shemaiah prophesied during the reign of Rehoboam when the latter mustered his army in hopes of regaining his sovereignty over the Northern Kingdom. Shemaiah warned him not to wage war.

18. Elijah: Elijah, a native of Gilead, prophesied and brought miracles in the kingdom of Ephraim during the reigns of King Ahab and his son Ahaziah. When Ahab, influenced by his wife Jezebel, had given himself to the worship of the Phoenician god Baal, Elijah's emergence was sudden and dramatic. He appeared upon the scene and predicted a drought as a penalty for the introduction of the Phoenician cult into Israel. Then followed the scene at Mount Carmel, demonstrating the supreme power of God and the impotence of Baal (1 Kings 18).

Aside from the patriarchs, Elijah is the most outstanding of the prophets who left no written works. According to the Prophet Malachi, Elijah will usher in the Messianic era: "And he shall turn the hearts of the fathers to the children, and the hearts of the children to their fathers" (Malachi 3:24).

The rabbis differed as to Elijah's origin. Some believed that he came from Gad, while others traced him to the tribe of Benjamin. Some thought he was a priest and even identified him with Pinchas (*Genesis Rabbah* 71:4; Talmud, *Bava Metzia* 114).

Of all biblical figures, Elijah the Prophet has

been singled out to become the beloved miracle-maker of Jewish legends. The Bible suggests that Elijah did not die. He was walking with his disciple Elisha, when he suddenly ascended heavenward in a chariot of fire (2 Kings 2:11).

19. **Micaiah, son of Imlah:** In the days of King Ahab, Micaiah was the only true prophet among the four hundred court prophets who told the king whatever he wished to hear (1 Kings 22:8). According to the sages (*Seder Olam*), it was Micaiah who disguised himself with a headband and ashes and prophesied that Ahab would fall in battle: "Because you have let go out of your hand the man whom I had devoted to destruction, therefore your life shall go for his life" (1 Kings 20:35–43). Imprisoned for this, though later freed and brought before Ahab and Jehoshaphat, he continued to prophesy the defeat of their enemies (2 Chronicles 18:24–27).

20. **Obadiah:** Obadiah lived toward the end of the era of the First Temple and prophesied the downfall of Edom. He also prophesied that the ruins of Israel would be rebuilt; that Israel would possess Mount Seir, the field of Ephraim, and the field of Samariah; and that the territory of the tribe of Benjamin would extend to Gilead, at which time "saviors shall come up on Mount Zion to judge the mount of Esau, and the kingdom shall be God's" (Obadiah: 19:21).

The rabbis identified the prophet with Obadiah, the overseer of the royal household, who lived in the days of King Ahab and hid and maintained one

hundred prophets sought by the wrathful Queen
Jezebel (1 Kings 18:3; Talmud, *Sanhedrin* 39b).

21. **Hanani, the Seer:** Hanani rebuked Asa, King of
Judah, for relying upon the King of Aram when in
danger, and not upon God (2 Chronicles 16:7–10).

22. **Jehu, son of Hanani:** Prophesying during the
reign of Asa, Jehu declared that Baasa, rule of the
Northern Kingdom, would suffer Jeroboam's fate.
Later, the prophet rebuked Jehoshaphat for becoming an ally of Ahab. Jehu wrote the chronicles
of Jehoshaphat (2 Chronicles 20:34).

23. **Azariah, son of Oded:** Azariah persuaded Asa to
remove the idols, to renovate the Temple, and
reform the government. Under his influence, Asa
renewed the covenant between the people and God
(2 Chronicles 15:1–19).

24. **Jahaziel, the Levite, son of Zechariah:** He en-
couraged Jehoshaphat in his wars against Ammon,
Moab, and Seir (2 Chronicles 20:14–19).

25. **Eliezer, son of Dodavahu of Mareshah:** A native
of Mareshah in Judah, he opposed the pact between Jehoshaphat, King of Judah, and Ahaziah,
King of Israel. Jehoshaphat paid no attention to his
words and sent ships to Eziongeber. These were
smashed (2 Chronicles 20:37).

26. **Elisha:** The son of Shaphat, Elisha was the
disciple and successor of Elijah, the Prophet. Elijah came upon Elisha while the latter was plowing

and threw his mantle over him, signifying that Elisha would ultimately succeed him (1 Kings 19:16–21).

Elisha had a remarkable career, performing more miracles than even Elijah. He spread out the mantle of his master and crossed the Jordan dry-shod (2 Kings 2:8); he purified the fountain in Jericho (2 Kings 19–22); he set bears upon children who mocked him (2 Kings 2:23–24); he miraculously increased a widow's supply of oil (2 Kings 4:1–7); he foretold the birth of the Shunamite woman's son and when the boy died, brought him to life again (2 Kings 4:8–37); he made poisonous pottage edible (2 Kings 4:38–41); he cured Naaman, the Syrian, of leprosy (2 Kings 5:1–19); and he prophesied the annihilation of the house of Ahab (2 Kings 8:1–10). Even after Elisha's death, miracles took place because of him: a dead man thrown into the prophet's grave was restored to life (2 Kings 13:20,21).

According to *Seder Olam*, the prophets mentioned in 2 Chronicles 24:19 are Elisha and Jonah: "Yet He sent prophets to them, to bring them back to the Lord; and they admonished them, but they would not give ear."

27. **Jonah, son of Amitta:** According to the Book of Jonah, the prophet was sent to the people of Nineveh to make them repent of their evildoing. According to rabbinic interpretation, Jonah refused to obey God's command, not wishing to help Israel's enemies repent and thereby make Israel the more culpable in God's sight. Thinking that God's Presence was only to be found in the Land of Israel, Jonah fled the country (*Yalkut Shimoni*, Exodus). However, in the end he was forced to

come to Nineveh and rouse its inhabitants to repentance.

28. Hosea, son of Beeri: Hosea prophesied from the
days of Uzziah until the beginning of the reign of
Hezekiah. He reproved the people for their depravity and their contentment with mere Temple
ritual; what was needed was knowledge of God and
the meaning of truth, loving-kindness, and the tradition. Hosea was pessimistic about the future of
the people of Judah and opposed the institution of
monarchy.

29. Amos: A farmer from Tekoah in Judah, he was
an innovator who markedly influenced succeeding
prophets. He preached the need for kindness and
compassion between man and nations. Foreseeing
the bitter end of the kingdom of Ephraim, Amos
anticipated the happy return of the exiles to their
homeland.

The rabbis declared (Talmud, *Makkot* 23b) that
Amos reduced all of the commandments of the
Torah to one: "For thus says the Lord unto the
Israel: Seek you Me, and live" (Amos 5:4).

30. Amoz: According to the sages, he was the brother
of King Amaziah (Talmud, *Megillah* 10) and the
father of the Prophet Isaiah. He reproved Amaziah
for importuning the gods of Edom. He was opposed
to the military alliance between the Kingdoms of
Judah and Ephraim (2 Chronicles 25:7–9).

31. Oded: Oded prophesied in Samaria during the
reign of Ahab, King of Judah, and Pekah, son of

Remaliah, King of Israel. When the children of Israel returned from Judah with numerous prisoners, the prophet went out and urged them in God's name to restore their captives to their native land. His words had a telling effect and the leaders of Ephraim did not bring any captives back to Samaria.

32. Isaiah, son of Amoz: Isaiah prophesied from the year of Uzziah's death (Isaiah 6:1) until the beginning of Manasseh's reign. Isaiah inveighed against luxury (Isaiah 3:18–23), social inequity and pride (Isaiah 2:17), and the levity (chapter 22) that led men to seek military aid from foreign nations. Isaiah was the first prophet to declare that idolatry and evil would one day cease to exist (chapter 27) as a result of reformation on the part of the people.

The sages declared that Isaiah was the greatest of the prophets (*Yalkut Shimoni*, Isaiah, para. 385).

33. Micah, the Morashtite: Prophesying in the days of Ahaz and Hezekiah, Micah spoke out against the social ills of his time, maintaining that they would bring about the nation's downfall. According to the Talmud (*Makkot* 23b), Micah reduced God's commandments to three: It has been told you, O man, what is good, and what God wants of you: only to do justly, love mercy, and walk humbly with your God (Micah 6:8).

34. Joel, son of Pethuel: The locust plague that took place during the lifetime of this prophet served as the symbol of the awesome events that would precede the coming of the so-called "day of the Lord" when God would judge all nations. These events would also cause the people to repent. According to the philosopher Maimonides, Joel received the tradition from Micah, the Prophet.

35. Nachum, the Elkoshite: Nachum lived during the reign of King Masasseh, according to the sages, and prophesied the destruction of Nineveh. In the Bible, Assyria is the embodiment of an evil nation; the fall of its capital, Nineveh, symbolizes the victory of Divine justice.

36. Uriah, son of Shemaiah: A native of Jiriath-yearim, Uriah prophesied during the reign of Je-hoiakim. He fled to Egypt from the anger of the king and his officers, only to be captured and killed there.

37. Habbakuk: According to the sages (*Seder Olam* 10), Habbakuk prophesied during the reign of King Manasseh. In his book, Habbakuk poses the question of the suffering of the innocent contrasted with the prosperity of the wicked, symbolized by the Chaldeans. The answer that God gives him is that the fall of the wicked is imminent.

38. Zephaniah: Prophesying during the reign of King Josiah, Zephaniah fought against the last vestiges of idolatry and against ethical and social depravity. The sages taught that Zephaniah was one of the three prominent prophets of his age, the other two being Jeremiah and Huldah. Zephaniah prophesied the punishment of the wicked followed by the universal acceptance of God. At that time, the remnant of Judah will be redeemed.

39. **Jeremiah, son of Hilkiah:** Jeremiah prophesied during the reign of King Josiah and continued until some time after the exile of the inhabitants of Jerusalem to Egypt. He vigorously opposed the Judean pact with Egypt against Babylon and prophesied that as a result of it, the city would be destroyed and the people sent into exile (chapter 21).

Jeremiah fought for the observance of the commandments of the Torah. He bitterly protested Sabbath desecration (Jeremiah 17:24), idolatry (7:31), false prophecy (14:14–16), and Israel's placing its trust in humans rather than in God (17:5).

The sages taught that Jeremiah wrote not only his own book, but the Books of Kings and Lamentations as well (Talmud, *Bava Batra* 15a).

40. **Ezekiel, the son of Buzi:** One of the greatest prophets, Ezekiel prophesied in Babylon, where he had been exiled with the captivity of Jehoiachin. Wrathfully, he elaborates on the sins of Israel, both in their own land and in the exile. He prophesies God's revenge upon the wicked, but also envisions the "dry bones" rising again. As a priest, Ezekiel depicts an idealized Temple ritual in glowing colors.

More than any other prophet, Ezekiel stressed the fact that all people are able to repent and that an individual is judged only for his own actions and not those of his ancestors or descendants.

41. Neriah: According to the Talmud, *Megillah* 14b, Neriah was the father of Baruch, student and secretary-scribe of Jeremiah. In the Book of Jeremiah (36:4), Neriah witnesses the appointment of his son as scribe to Jeremiah.

42. Baruch, son of Neriah: The scribe and student of Jeremiah, Baruch "wrote from the mouth of Jeremiah all the words of God which He had spoken to him, upon a roll of a book" (Jeremiah 36:4). According to Maimonides, Baruch received the tradition from the Prophet Jeremiah.

43. Seraiah, son of Neriah: According to the rabbis, a prophet's disciple is also a prophet (Rashi, Talmud, *Megillah* 15), and such was Seraiah, of whom the Bible says: "The word which Jeremiah the prophet commanded Seraiah the son of Neriah, the son of Mahseiah" (Jeremiah 51:59).

44. Mahseiah: Mahseiah was the father of Neriah and grandfather of Baruch, the scribe of Jeremiah (Jeremiah 32:12).

45. Haggai: Haggai urged Zerubbabel and the rest of the people to rebuild the Temple, which lay in ruins. His words were effective, and the Temple was completed in the sixth year of Darius's reign (Ezra 5:1,2). Haggai also prophesied that "the glory of this latter house shall be greater than that of the former" (Haggai 2:9), a prophecy that was eventually fully realized.

46. Zechariah, son of Berechiah: Like Haggai, Zechariah urged the Jews who had returned to Zion to complete the building of the Temple. He was able to revive the spirit of those who had become discouraged by hardship. Zechariah declared that belief in God would spread throughout the nations and that idolatry would cease. His visions were unique among the prophets in that an angel helped to interpret them.

47. **Malachi:** The sages taught that Malachi was the last of the prophets and was none other than Ezra, the Scribe (Talmud, *Megillah* 15a). Malachi attacked the priests for desecrating the altar and not taking their holy mission seriously. He also inveighed against intermarriage with foreign women and stressed the sanctity of marital bonds. Finally, Malachi also foretold the coming of Elijah: "Behold, I will send you Elijah the Prophet before the coming of the great and terrible day of the Lord" (Malachi 3:23).

48. **Mordecai:** Mordecai lived in Shushan and reared Esther, his cousin. He played an instrumental role in saving the Jews from Persian persecution by the evil man Haman. The rabbis identified Mordecai with Mordecai Bilshan, who is mentioned in the Bible as one of the Jews who returned to Judah from Babylon in the days of Zerubbabal (Ezra 2:2, Nehemiah 7:7).

11

Seven Prophetesses

In addition to the forty-eight prophets, according to Rashi, there are seven prophetesses. Here is a listing and a brief summary of each of them:

1. **Sarah:** In the Bible it is written: "Haran, the father of Milcah, and the father of Iscah" (Genesis 11:29). Rabbi Isaac identified Iscah as Sarah, because she perceived (in Hebrew, *sachta*) by the Divine spirit, as it is written: "God said to Abraham . . . all that Sarah says to you, listen to her voice" (Genesis 21:12) (Talmud, *Megillah* 14a).

2. **Miriam:** Miriam, sister of Moses, is specifically referred to in the Bible as a prophetess: "And Miriam the prophetess . . . took a timbrel" (Exodus 15:20). Yet another allusion to her role as a prophet can be found in the Book of Numbers. Criticizing Moses for having married a Cushite woman, Miriam said: "Has God indeed spoken only with Moses? Has he not spoken with us?" (Numbers 12:2).

According to the rabbis, Miriam began to prophesy in Egypt before the birth of her brother Moses, when she said: "My mother shall give birth to a son who will save Israel." When Moses was born, the room was filled with light and her father kissed her forehead and said: "My daughter, your prophecy has been fulfilled." However, when Moses was cast into the Nile, Amram struck Miriam and said: "Where is your prophecy now?" This is the meaning of the phrase "Her sister stood at a distance to learn"—to learn what would become of her prophecy (Talmud, *Megillah* 14a).

3. **Deborah:** The only thing we know about Deborah's personal life is the name of her husband, Lapidot. "She led Israel at that time" is how the Bible records it. "Deborah the prophetess used to sit under the palm tree of Deborah and the Israelites would come to her for judgment" (Judges 4:4).

Although Deborah was not called upon to foretell the future, the Bible commentator Kimchi asserts that she is described as a prophet in the Book of Judges because she was inspired to grapple with the great difficulties of the hour. She led a successful Israelite revolt against Canaanite domination in the northern part of the country. The story of her triumph is told in a stirring ode attributed to Deborah (Judges 5:1–31).

4. **Hannah:** In the Bible it is written: "And Hannah prayed and said: My heart exults in God, my horn is exalted in the Lord" (1 Samuel 2:1). "My horn is exalted" and not "my pitcher is exalted." According to the sages, this means that the dynasties of King David and King Solomon, who were anointed with oil from a horn, would be prolonged, while the

dynasties of Saul and Jehu, who were anointed with oil from a pitcher, would not be prolonged" (Talmud, *Megillah* 14a).

Hannah's entire prayer is interpreted as a prophecy referring to Sennacherib, Nebuchadnezzar, and Haman (*Yalkut Shimoni*, Samuel).

5. **Abigail:** The Bible records that Abigail prophesied to David: "God will certainly make my lord a sure house . . . and it shall come to pass, when the Lord shall have done to my lord according to all the good that He has spoken concerning you, and shall have appointed you prince over Israel . . ." (1 Samuel 25:28–31).

6. **Huldah:** The wife of Shallum, she was keeper of the royal wardrobe, living near the courts of learning in Jerusalem during the reign of King Josiah (2 Kings 22:14). When the "Book of Law" was found and read before the king, he sent for Huldah to inquire about the book. She told the king that God had decreed to punish the people because of the sins of earlier generations, but because Josiah had repented, the punishment would not come upon him. "Neither shall your eyes see all the evil which I will bring upon this place" (2 Kings 22:20).

7. **Esther:** The rabbis regarded Esther as a prophet because the Bible says of her: "Esther put on her royal apparel" (Esther 5:1). This was interpreted to mean that she was clothed with the Divine Spirit, as it is written: "Then the spirit clothed Amasai" (1 Chronicles 12:19; Talmud, *Megillah* 14b).

12

Seven Heathen Prophets

Rabbi Isaac, in the *Song of Songs Rabbah* 2:13, is quoted as saying: "Until the tabernacle was erected there was prophecy among the heathen; when the tabernacle was erected, prophecy ceased among them. Yet did not Balaam the son of Beor prophesy? Yes, but only because he prophesied good for Israel" (*Song of Songs Rabbah* 2:12).

The following are the seven heathen prophets, according to the accounting of the Vilna Gaon.

1. **Beor:** The father of Balaam (Numbers 22:5), he was considered a prophet in accordance with the rabbinic ruling that wherever the name of a prophet's father is mentioned, both father and son are prophets.

2. **Balaam:** This heathen prophet was invited by Balak, King of Moab, to curse the Israelites when they approached his country during their wanderings in the wilderness. Divinely inspired, Balaam uttered blessings in place of curses (Numbers 22:5).

According to the rabbis, Balaam was superior to even Moses in three respects: Moses did not know who spoke to him, while Balaam did; Moses did not know beforehand when he would be spoken to while Balaam did know; and God did not speak to Moses unless he was standing, while Balaam was addressed even when he was lying down (*Sifre Deuteronomy* 357).

However, Balaam had some bad traits, according to the rabbis. He was described in *Pirke Avot* 5:9 as having an evil eye, a haughty spirit, and excessive pride. Balaam also did his best to make the Israelites break faith with God and sought to destroy the entire people by having them commit harlotry (Numbers 31:16). Because of Balaam's actions, the rabbis declared, God took the power of prophecy away from the heathens (*Numbers Rabbah* 2:1).

3. **Job:** The sages maintained that Job lived either during Jacob's lifetime or at the time of the Exodus from Egypt (Talmud, *Bava Batra* 15). The rabbis differed as to whether Job served God out of fear or out of love. The majority felt that he did serve out of love (*Tosefta Sotah* 7:1; Talmud, *Sotah* 27b). Some sages maintain that Job was punished because he, together with Balaam, was a counselor of Pharaoh and when Balaam advised Pharaoh to cast the children of Israel into the Nile, he did not disapprove (Talmud, *Sotah* 11, and Talmud, *Sanhedrin* 106).

4. **Eliphaz:** Eliphaz was one of Job's friends (2:11). In the fourth chapter of the Book of Job, Eliphaz speaks of the prophetic vision that came upon him:

"Now a word was secretly brought to me, and my ear received a whisper. In thoughts from the visions of the night, when deep sleep falls on men, fear came upon me, and trembling, all of my bones were made to shake. Then a spirit passed before my face, that made the hair of my flesh stand up. A form was before my eyes. I heard a still voice" (Job 4:12–16).

5. **Bildad, the Shuhite:** He appears in the Book of Job 2:11. He condemns Job's words as a mighty wind and firmly maintains the traditional belief in retributive justice.

6. **Zophar, the Naamatite:** He appears in the Book of Job 2:11.

7. **Elihu:** The son of Barachel, Elihu was the youngest of Job's four friends (Job 32:2). He declared that a Divine revelation came upon him while he was sleeping: "For God speaks in one way, yea in two, though man does not perceive it. In a dream, in a vision of the night, when deep sleep falls on man, in slumberings upon the bed" (Job 33:14–15). The rabbis deduced from this verse that "the heathen prophets were spoken to only at nighttime" (*Numbers Rabbah* 20:9 and *Leviticus Rabbah* 1).

III

The Fifteen Literary Prophets: A Summary of Their Books

13

The Major Prophets

Isaiah

This chapter will summarize each book of the literary prophets. It is intended to provide a short but concise overview of the prophet himself, his place and time, and the contents of his book and its messages.

Isaiah and His Family

The name Isaiah, in Hebrew *Yeshayahu*, means "salvation of God." This is a name in total harmony with Isaiah's teachings; Isaiah was the first prophet to declare that idolatry and evil would one day cease to exist (chapter 27) as a result of a reformation on the part of the people. According to the Book of Isaiah, Isaiah was a married man, and his wife was called by the title "the prophetess." He also had at least two sons, She'ar yashuv and Maher-shalal-hash-baz. The latter son, whose name means "the spoil speeds and the prey hastens," was so named as a warning on the fate of Damascus and Samarai, representing Syria and the kingdom of Israel, whose wealth was to be carried away by Assyria.

Of a noble family, his father was Amoz, who according to tradition was the brother of Amaziah, a king of Judah. Isaiah was closely connected with the royal court and, especially under Hezekiah, was prominent in public affairs.

Isaiah prophesied in Jerusalem from the time of the death of Uzziah until the middle of King Hezekiah's reign (740–701 B.C.E.). He received the call to his prophetic mission in the closing year of the life of Uzziah or Azariah (740–739 B.C.E.) and his activities continued throughout the reigns of the succeeding kings of Judah, Jothan, Ahaz, and Hezekiah. His call to prophecy is a most beautiful and graphic one, in which fiery angels called "seraphim" make their appearance. But, like most prophets, he is at first reluctant to accept the role of a prophet, feeling that his own spiritual shortcomings create an insurmountable barrier between him and the Divine call. Here is Isaiah's calling in his own words:

> In the year that Uzziah died I saw God sitting on a high throne and lifted up, and God's train filled the temple. Above God stood the seraphim, each one had six wings . . . And one called to the other saying: "Holy, holy, holy is the Lord of hosts, the whole earth is filled with God's Presence." And the posts of the door were moved at the voice of them that called, and the house was filled with smoke. Then I said: "Woe is me, for I am undone. Because

I am a man of unclean lips and I dwell in the midst of a people of unclean lips. For my eyes have seen the King, the Lord of Hosts." Then one of the seraphim flew in to me, with a glowing stone in his hand, which he had taken with the tongs from off the altar. And he touched my mouth with it, and said: "Lo, this has touched your lips. And your iniquity is taken away, and your sin expiated." And I heard the voice of God saying: "Whom shall I send and who will go for us?" Then I said: "Here am I, send me." (Isaiah 6:1–8)

Composition and Authorship of the Book

The Book of Isaiah consists of sixty-six chapters, embodying a variety of oracles on Judah and Israel as well as on other nations, such as Egypt, Babylon, Moab, Edom, Tyre, Syria, and Arabia. The book spans the period of pre-exile when Judah had yet to be conquered, exile when the Judeans were dispersed to Babylon, and post-exile when the Israelites returned to their country to rebuild it. The sections of the book that deal with these three time periods often display different styles and tones and have led Bible critics to the conclusion that the Book of Isaiah itself did not come from the pen of one single man but is the result of a composite of prophets. Scholars generally divide the book into two main sections: chapters 1–39 and chapters 40–66. The authorship of the latter has been ascribed to a second ("deutero") Isaiah writing during the time of the Babylonian exile. Some modern biblical scholars maintain that a third Isaiah, a Palestinian prophet, assumed to be active after the return from Babylonian captivity, wrote chapters 56–66. The time frame for the Babylonian captivity is more than a century after the events described in chapters 1–39 of the Book of Isaiah.

Subject Matter and Mission

In subject matter, the Book of Isaiah is divisible into chapters. Chapters 1–12 (c. 761–740 B.C.E.) deal with prophecies to Israel and Judah and promises of a glorious future. Chapters 13–23 deal with Isaiah's visions concerning other nations; chapters 24–27 are apocalyptic prophecies on the future Day of Judgment; and chapters 28–33 deal with the campaign of Sennacherib, King of Assyria. Chapters 34–35 are a short apocalypse incorporating a vision of Edom, while chapters 36–39 are historical chapters in prose describing the march of Sennacherib and the mission of Merodach Baladan. Chapters 40–66 are chapters of consolation and promise of future redemption. This is interrupted by the vision (52:13–53:12) of the Suffering Servant, interpreted by most Jewish commentators to be referring to collective Israel, but considered by Christian missionaries to be foretelling the coming of Jesus as the Messiah.

Isaiah began his prophetic career at a time when there was abundant prosperity in Judea, vast stores of silver and gold. He witnessed the growth of huge estates, the oppression of the poor, the pursuit of perverse pleasure, and the spread of idolatry. He was convinced that all of this could not continue with impunity and that ultimately the people of Israel would have to be accountable to God for their actions. If they persisted, Isaiah warned, God would destroy both of the kingdoms of Judah and Israel.

Isaiah appeared at a critical juncture in the history of the Jewish people. The second half of the eighth century witnessed the collapse of the Israelite Kingdom under the forces of Assyria (722 B.C.E.), while the holy city of Jerusalem, the capital of Judea, was besieged by Sennacherib's army in 701 B.C.E. Isaiah's entire career was devoted to impressing upon his people that the world was based on morality and justice and that leading an ethical life was the only way to avert complete disaster.

Little is known about the last days of Isaiah. There is no written record of his dying or the cause of his death, although a rabbinic tradition attributes it to King Manasseh.

Place in the Canon

The location of the Book of Isaiah in the biblical canon is, according to the Talmud, after the Book of Ezekiel. In the printed editions of the Hebrew Bible, as well as according to the *Masorah*, Isaiah's place is the first of the Later Prophets, immediately following the Second Book of Kings, the last Book of the Early Prophets.

Major Concepts and Teachings

1. The Covenental Relationship between God and the Israelites: God had chosen Israel from among all of the nations to be His special people. This special pact was to be an eternal one, and Israel was to forever be the chosen people. Israel was also told that its mission was to be a light for the nations, enlightening all those who are blind to the truth (Isaiah 42:6). As a light of the nations, Israel was chosen to be God's agent and God's partner, helping Him show the entire world that what God wants from humanity is the highest ethical behavior.

2. The Universal God: Although God is the God of Israel and has a special relationship with the Israelites, God is also the Creator of the entire Universe, and His glory totally pervades it. One day there will be a Day of Judgment when all people will come to know and understand that there is only One God, Ruler over all.

3. World Peace and the Messianic Era: Isaiah had a vision in which he saw a time when "nation shall not lay up sword against nation, neither shall people learn war anymore" (Isaiah 2:4). He also foretold of a Messianic time when "the wolf shall dwell with the lamb, and the leopard lie down with the kid" (Isaiah 11:6).

4. Ritual's purpose was to lead a person to promote social justice: Isaiah says (Isaiah 1:16–17) that

God cannot endure the sacrificial ceremonies that have built up as solemn assemblies around such sacred times as the appearance of the new moon or the coming of the Sabbath. Rather, what God wants for the Israelites is that their sacrifices be the magnifying glass through which the people could see more clearly the ethical demands that God placed on the people. Such demands include aiding the orphan, defending the cause of the widow, and devoting oneself to justice. Thus, the purpose of sacrifice was a means and not an end in and of itself. The people, in Isaiah's opinion, were punished by their defeat by Assyria and Babylon precisely because they had confused the ends with the means, failing to understand that God wanted those who called themselves religious to be both ethical and ritually observant.

Interestingly, Isaiah's stress on social justice was so well-known in the Western World that President Franklin Delano Roosevelt nicknamed the Jewish Supreme Court Justice Louis Brandeis, "Isaiah."

Isaiah in Rabbinic Literature

The following is a cross-section of rabbinic citations related to Isaiah.

1. Isaiah was a descendant of Judah and Tamar (Talmud, *Sotah* 10b).

2. Isaiah's father was a prophet and the brother of King Amaziah (Talmud, *Megillah* 15a).

3. Isaiah was distinguished from all other prophets in that he received his communications directly from God and not through an intermediary (*Leviticus Rabbah* 10).

4. In the order of greatness, Isaiah is placed immediately after Moses by the sages. In some respects he surpasses even Moses, for he reduced the commandments to six: honesty in dealing, sincerity in speech, refusal of illicit gain, absence of corruption, aversion for bloody deeds, and contempt for evil (Talmud, *Makkot* 24a).

5. The chief merit of Isaiah's prophecies is their ability to console others. The Prophet Ezekiel's consoling addresses compared with Isaiah's are as the utterances of a villager to the speech of a courtier (Talmud, *Chagiga* 14a).

6. It is related in the Talmud that Rabbi Simeon ben Azzai found in Jerusalem an account wherein it was written that Manasseh killed Isaiah. Manasseh said to Isaiah: "Moses your master said, 'There shall no man see God and live' (Exodus 32:20); but you have said, 'I saw God seated upon His throne'" (Isaiah 6:1) and went on to point out other contradictions. Isaiah then said: "I know that he will not accept my explanations; why should I increase his guilt?" He then uttered the Unpronounceable Name, a cedar tree opened, and Isaiah disappeared within it. Then Manasseh ordered the cedar to be sawed, and when the saw reached his mouth Isaiah died. Thus was he punished for hav-

ing said, "I dwell in the midst of a people of unclean lips" (Talmud, *Yevamot* 49b).

Notable Quotations

1. I the Lord have called you in righteousness, and have taken hold of your hand. I have kept you and set you for a covenant of the people, for a light unto the nations (Isaiah 42:6).

2. For the mountains may depart, and the hills may be removed. But My kindness shall not depart from you, neither shall My covenant of peace be removed, says the Lord that has compassion on you (Isaiah 54:10).

3. And all your children shall be taught of the Lord, and great shall be the peace of your children (Isaiah 54:13).

4. They that wait for the Lord shall renew their strength. They shall mount up with wings as eagles; they shall run, and not be weary; they shall walk and not faint (Isaiah 40:31).

5. Whom shall one teach knowledge? And whom shall one make to understand the message? Them that are weaned from milk, and those that are drawn from the breasts. For it is precept by precept, line by line, here a little, there a little (Isaiah 28:9–10).

6. Thus says the Lord, the King of Israel, and his Redeemer the Lord of hosts. I am the first, and I am the last, and beside Me, there is no God (Isaiah 54:6).

7. Your new moons and your appointed seasons, My soul hates. They are a burden to Me. I am weary to bear them (Isaiah 1:14).

8. Comfort you, comfort you, My people, says the Lord (Isaiah 40:1).

9. Hark! One says, "Proclaim." And he says: "What shall I proclaim?" "All flesh is grass, and all the goodness thereof is as the flower of the field. The grass withers and the flowers fade when a wind of the Lord blows upon them. Surely the people are like grass. The grass withers and the flowers fade, but the word of our God shall endure forever (Isaiah 40:6–7). [Note: These verses often appear in clergy manuals as a suggested text for funerals.]

10. Awake, awake, put on your strength, O Zion. Put on your beautiful garments, O Jerusalem, the holy city. For henceforth there shall no more come to you the uncircumcised and the unclean (Isaiah 52:1).

11. For this to Me is like the waters of Noah: As I swore that the waters of Noah nevermore would flood the earth, so I swear that I will not be angry with you or rebuke you (Isaiah 54:9).

12. Arise, arise, for your light has dawned. The Presence of God has shone upon you (Isaiah 60:1).

13. And new moon after new moon, and Sabbath after Sabbath, all flesh shall come to worship Me (Isaiah 66:23).

14. He was despised, shunned by men, a man of suffering, familiar with disease. As one who hid his face from us, he was despised and held of no account. Yet it was our sickness that he was bearing, our suffering that he endured. We accounted him plagued, smitten and afflicted by God. But he was wounded because of our sins, crushed because of our transgressions. He bore the chastisement, made us whole, and by his bruises we were healed (Isaiah 53:3–5). [Note: The term "servant of the Lord" first appears in Isaiah 42:2–4. In this passage, the Servant is portrayed as suffering vicariously. This passage has evoked considerable controversy. The Servant of the Lord has been identified with the people of Israel, the Messiah, and the Prophet Isaiah himself. In the Christian tradition, he has often been identified with Jesus.]

15. Nation shall not lift up sword against nation, neither shall they learn war anymore (Isaiah 2:4). [Note: These words adorn the walls across the street from the United Nations in New York.]

16. For out of Zion shall go forth the Torah, and the word of God from Jerusalem (Isaiah 2:3). [Note: This verse is used liturgically as part of the introduction to the service for taking out the Torah scroll on weekdays and on the Sabbath and festivals.]

Jeremiah

Life and Character of Jeremiah

Of all of the prophets of the Bible, Jeremiah is likely to be considered the most self-revealing. His name itself in Hebrew, *Yirmiyahu*, means "may God lift up." Nothing is known of Jeremiah's childhood and youth, except that he did not marry (Jeremiah 16:1–4). Since young men in those days usually married early in life, the fact that Jeremiah did not may indicate that he felt himself completely devoted to his God-given mission, leaving no room for a life or family. None have told so much about themselves as he has, revealing an array of emotions that allows the reader to feel his poignant sorrow toward an Israelite people that had gone astray: "O my suffering, O my suffering! How I writhe! Oh, the walls of my heart. My heart moans within me . . ." (Jeremiah 4:20).

Jeremiah was the son of Hilkiah, of a priestly family in Anathote (southwest of Jerusalem). We learn in the first chapter of his book that Jeremiah was predestined to be a prophet:

> And the word of God came to me, saying: Before I formed you in the belly I knew you, and before you came forth out of the womb I sanctified you; I have appointed you a prophet for the nations . . . Then God put forth His hand and touched my mouth and God said to me: Behold, I have put My words in your mouth. (Jeremiah 1:1, 4, 5)

Jeremiah, showing a sense of humility and self-distrust of his own ability, proceeds to tell God that he is but a child and cannot speak. But God reassures him in these words:

> "Say not I am a child. For to whomsoever I shall send you, you shall go, and whatsoever I shall command you shall speak. Then God put forth His hand and touched my mouth, and God said to me: Behold I have put My words in your mouth . . . (Jeremiah 1:6, 9).

Background of the Times

The period of Jeremiah's ministry extends from the thirteenth year of Josiah's reign (625 B.C.E.) until after the destruction of the Temple and the overthrow of the Judean State in 586. Jeremiah began to prophesy in Jerusalem about twenty years after the death of Isaiah. More is known about his life and teachings than about any other prophet, since the book of Jeremiah contains much historical and biographical material.

King Josiah had come to the throne at the young age of eight years, after the fifty-two-year reign of his father, Manasseh. He did not succeed him directly but followed his brother Amon, who was assassinated after being on the throne less than two years (637 B.C.E.). Manasseh's reign had been marked by political and religious regression. The country was forced to submit to the rule of Assyria and the people reverted to idolatry, augury, divination, and even human sacrifice. King Manasseh himself even made his own son pass through the fire of Molech.

In the eighteenth year of King Josiah's reign (621 B.C.E.), the Temple was being repaired and a copy of a book of the Torah was found by Hilkiah, the High Priest. The book (some scholars assert that it was the Book of Deuteronomy) was read to King Josiah, who was deeply stirred by its contents, which resulted in his initiating the cleansing and purification of the Temple. However, the people continued to revert to their idolatrous practices

In his book, Jeremiah witnesses the fall of Nineveh and the annihilation of the Assyrian Empire in 606 B.C.E. He also witnesses the death of King Josiah in 605 and lives through the two sieges of Jerusalem in 597 and 586 B.C.E., with the attendant destruction of the Jewish state and the transportation of the greater portion of his people to "the rivers of Babylon." After the fall of Jerusalem, Jeremiah was forcibly taken into Egypt by those who fled the wrath of the Babylon King Nebuchadnezzar.

Tradition reports that the king had instructed his general to treat Jeremiah with consideration and kindness. But the prophet insisted on sharing the hardships that were inflicted on his people. Afterward, Jeremiah was killed in Egypt, where he had continued his fiery speeches.

Jeremiah's influences on his people may well have been greater after his death than before. Arrest and imprisonment were his lot when alive. After his death, the exiled Judeans in Babylon religiously meditated upon his lessons and were guided by them. Jeremiah's influence is clearly reflected in the visions of Ezekiel, who became a prophet in Babylon and prepared his fellow exiles for King Nebuchadnezzar's destruction of Jerusalem.

Composition and Authorship

The Book of Jeremiah is the longest of the prophetic books, even though it has fifty-two chapters, fourteen less than that of the Book of Isaiah. Jeremiah's dictations to his faithful secretary Baruch were written down upon a scroll of leather, which the King of Judah slashed with a knife and burned. Jeremiah then ordered his scribe to take another scroll and write therein all of the words of the book that the king had burned.

Subject Matter and Book Summary

The following is a synopsis of the events in the Book of Jeremiah, chapter by chapter:

CHAPTERS 1–20—PROPHECIES BETWEEN JEREMIAH'S CALL (625 B.C.E.) AND THE FOURTH YEAR OF JEHOIAKIM (604 B.C.E.)

1:1–19	The call of Jeremiah to prophecy
2:1–4:4	Indictment of the nation's sin
4:5–6:30	Description of the coming disaster "from the north" (i.e., Babylon)
7:1–8:3	Temple sermons and appended sayings
8:4–9:21	The tragic ruin of an unmanageable people
9:22–10:25	Various sayings and an unmanageable people and their ruin
11:1-17	Jeremiah preaches on the broken covenant
11:18–12:6	Jeremiah is persecuted by his relatives and the townspeople
12:7–17	God expresses His sorrow for the delinquency of the Israelites
13:1–27	Symbol of the linen girdle and parable of the wine bottle
14:1–15:4	Drought in the land, a time of national calamity
15:5–16:21	Oracles and confessions

CHAPTERS 21–25:14—PROPHECIES CONCERNING THE KINGS OF JUDAH AND THE FALSE PROPHETS

CHAPTER 25:15–38— SUMMARY OF THE PROPHECIES AGAINST THE OTHER NATIONS, WHICH APPEAR IN CHAPTERS 46–51

CHAPTERS 26–28—PROPHECIES OF THE FALL OF JERUSALEM

CHAPTERS 32–44—HISTORY
OF THE TWO YEARS BEFORE THE
DOWNFALL OF THE JUDEAN STATE

Place in the Canon

Jeremiah is the book that follows the Book of Isaiah in the *Tanach*. It is the second book of the Latter Prophets.

Jeremiah's Style

The Book of Jeremiah is a combination of prose and poetry. Jeremiah's style is clear, concise, terse, and succinct. The images that he portrays are graphic and picturesque, and Jeremiah's own personal feelings, especially when he is filled with emotional distress, are described with precision and detail. Jeremiah is a true patriot with an intense love for his people, and the reader is treated to an outpouring of tenderness. Jeremiah identifies himself completely with the agonies of his people: "My bowels, my bowels. I writhe in pain! The chambers of my heart. My heart moans within me. I cannot hold my peace. Because you have heard, O my soul, the sound of the horn, the alarm of war" (Jeremiah 4:19).

Jeremiah's pathos, simplicity, and gentle appeal are evident in this early address, in which God is described as remembering Israel's love for Him in the past: "I remember for you the affection of your youth, the love of your espousals; how you went after Me in the wilderness, in a land that was unsown" (Jeremiah 2:1). Here we see the love relationship between God and the people of Israel, and the confidence that the Israelites displayed in God during the early stages of Israel's national existence.

Jeremiah is also known for his picturesque nature imagery. This is how Jeremiah describes the faithlessness of Israel: "For My people have committed two evils: they have forsaken Me, the fountain of living waters, and hewed them out cisterns, broken cisterns, that can hold no water" (Jeremiah 2:13).

Finally, Jeremiah's knowledge of animal life also abounds throughout the book, with graphic imagery related to the animal kingdom. Here is how Jeremiah describes the people of Israel who have gone astray: "You are a swift young camel traversing her ways. A wild ass used to the wilderness, that snuffs up the wind in her desire. Her lust, who can hinder it? All they that seek her will not tire themselves . . ." (Jeremiah 2:23–24).

Major Concepts and Teachings

1. God: Throughout his book Jeremiah continues to theologize, insisting first and foremost that God is the only One worthy of being worshiped. In contrast to the idols, God is all-knowing, all-seeing, and all powerful. God is the Lord of nature and is a universal Creator Who has the right to dispose of all nations as He wills. As the universal Creator, God orders all nations to submit to King Nebuchadnezzar (Jeremiah 27:5–9). God is also a God

of justice Who delights in righteousness while practicing acts of kindness on earth (Jeremiah 9:23). God is also a God Who rewards and punishes for the sin of profanation of His name (Jeremiah 16:17–18). Yet there is also a tender and merciful side to God's nature. Even though the people of Israel have sinned, God will remember the affection of better days when, early in their history, the people showed their unequivocal love by following Him in the wilderness (Jeremiah 2:2).

Finally, God is an omnipresent God Who can be approached even in exile. In the well-known letter to the exiles, the Prophet Jeremiah assures the exiled Israelites that if they seek God, they will find Him and that God would bring them back from their captivity (Jeremiah 29:12–14).

2. The Covenant between God and the Israelites: Jeremiah constantly alludes to the unbreakable bond and partnership—the covenant—between God and the children of Israel. God chose the Israelites to be His special people, and the Israelites accepted, thereby imposing special religious and ethical obligations upon themselves. Jeremiah begins his prophetic teaching by reminding the people of this unbreakable relationship: "Go and cry in the ears of Jerusalem, saying: Thus says God: I remember for you the affection of your youth, the love of your espousals, how you went after Me in the wilderness, in a land that was not sown" (Jeremiah 2:2).

The covenant is based on that which God originally made with the patriarch Abraham and renewed at the Exodus. In his book, Jeremiah singles out two items that are particularly pertinent to the keeping of the covenant. In the first, Jeremiah emphasizes (17:21–25) that the land will remain intact only if Israel keeps the Sabbath. The other, related to protection of the weak, emphasizes the freeing of the slaves after their six years of slavery, in accordance with the law in Exodus 21:2.

In chapter 31:31–33, mention is made of a new covenant that God will make with the House of Israel. Although no revelation is intended, the new covenant was intended to be more permanent than the old, because it will be inscribed directly onto the hearts of the people. Jeremiah makes the assertion that unlike in the past, Israel will henceforth remain faithful to God, while God in turn will never reject Israel.

3. God's message also extends to non-Israelites: At the beginning of his ministry, Jeremiah strikes the note of universalism: "I have appointed you a prophet unto all of the nations" (Jeremiah 1:5). Hence, the book contains a number of messages addressed to non-Israelites. In fact, from chapter 44 onward, the book is almost entirely concerned with other nations and only to a slight degree with Judah and Israel. Since Jeremiah teaches that the other nations, particularly Babylon, have been summoned by God to punish Judah for its sins, Jeremiah feels bitter toward them. He calls upon God to pour out his anger on the nations that do not know Him: "Pour out Your wrath upon the nations that do not know You, and upon the families that call not on Your name" (Jeremiah 10:25). [Note:

This verse has been incorporated into the Passover *Haggadah*, and is part of its recitation.]

On the other hand, Jeremiah predicts that the nations would be built up amidst the Judeans if they learn to swear by the name of God and attest to the fact that God alone rules the world: "And it shall come to pass, if they will diligently learn the ways of My people to swear by My name: 'As the Lord lives,' even as they taught My people to swear by Baal; then shall they be built up in the midst of My people." In chapter 16:19, Jeremiah anticipates that ultimately all people of all the nations will recognize God alone as the Ruler of the world.

In the final chapters of his book, Jeremiah prophesies the doom of several nations, including Moab, the Philistines, Ammon, and Elam. Interestingly, he at times expresses sympathy with them, and, in the case of Elam (Jeremiah 49:39), he tempers his prophecy against it by predicting its eventual restoration.

4. Jerusalem and the Temple are sacred to the Jewish people: In Jeremiah 3:17, the prophet declares: "At that time they shall call Jerusalem the throne of God; and all the nations shall be gathered to it, to the name of the Lord, to Jerusalem." With such a fixed connection between Jerusalem, the Temple, and the Israelites, it was not surprising that the people might have a sense of false security, knowing that the Temple was God's home. To combat this illusion, Jeremiah speaks out, saying to his people that the mere possession of the Temple in Jerusalem would not save the people from their apostasy: "Do not trust in lying words,

saying: 'The Temple of the Lord, the Temple of the Lord, the Temple of the Lord, are these' (Jeremiah 7:4). Jeremiah's prophecy that the Temple would be destroyed inflamed the people, who demanded his death. He was formally arraigned on a charge of treason and narrowly escaped, continuing to preach a message of doom to the Israelites.

5. Jeremiah and the exile of the Israelites: A most salient feature of the Book of Jeremiah is Jeremiah's constant and frequent prediction that the Judeans were headed for exile. Modern biblical scholars have often interpreted this fact to mean that Jeremiah had reached the stage of religious development where he saw that God could be worshiped outside of the Holy Land. Exile, they assert, allowed the people to understand that God was not attached to the land of Canaan and allowed them to diffuse their knowledge of God to the other nations.

Other commentators state that Jeremiah predicted exile not as something beneficial either to Israel or the other nations, but simply as a punishment for the apostasy of the Israelites. This punishment would be revoked as soon as Israel properly repented for its wrongdoings. In one of Jeremiah's early speeches (3:1), he poetically describes exile as a divorce between God and Israel: "If a man put divorce his way, and she go from him and become another man's wife, may he return to her again? Will not that land be greatly polluted? But you have played the harlot with many lovers . . ."

Another effect of the exile would be the repudiation of the doctrine of ancestral responsibility with the substitution of individual responsibility, according to which a person is punished only for his own sins and not for those of his parents. Jeremiah declares (31:28–29): "In those days they shall say no more: 'The fathers have eaten sour grapes, and the children's teeth are set on edge.' But every one shall die for his own transgression; every person that eats the sour grapes, his teeth shall be set on edge." This same proverb receives more comment in the next book that will be examined, namely, that of Ezekiel (18:2–4). The implication is that no more will it be assumed that children are punished for the sins of their parents, but there will be acknowledgement that when people are punished, it is for their own sins.

Finally, it is important to recall the fact that beyond the exile, Jeremiah looked forward and predicted a restoration to the land. In chapter 32 of his book, at the time when Jerusalem was under siege, Jeremiah purchases an estate in Anatothe from his kinsman, depositing the title deeds with his secretary Baruch, in the firm conviction that the Israelite nation would again return to its homeland. Not only from Babylon, but from all the countries of their exile, would the people of Israel be brought to dwell in their land. This fact is eloquently stated in Jeremiah 23:3–4, when God states: "I will gather the remnant of My flock out of all the countries to which I have driven them, and will bring them back to their folds, and they shall be fruitful and multiply. And I will set up shepherds over them, who shall feed them; and they shall fear no more, nor be dismayed, neither shall any be lacking . . ."

Jeremiah in Rabbinic Legend

There are many rabbinic references to Jeremiah of a legendary nature. Following is a listing of opinions related to the Book of Jeremiah in legend and lore:

1. Jeremiah was descended from Joshua and Rachab, the harlot (Talmud, *Megillah* 14b). They also pointed out many similarities between Jeremiah and Moses. Like Moses, he, too, prophesied to Israel for forty years; and he, too, was set upon by members of his own tribe and was saved from their hands. His love for Israel was great (*Yalkut Shimoni*, Jeremiah).

2. Jeremiah was born circumcised (*Avot de Rabbi Natan* 2:12) and already showed signs of his future calling when, as a newborn infant, he spoke in the voice of a youth and rebuked his mother for her unfaithfulness. He explained to his amazed mother that he was really rebuking the inhabitants of Jerusalem (*Pesikta Rabbata* 26:129).

3. Jeremiah was related to the prophetess Huldah. She preached to the women while Zephaniah, another contemporary prophet, was active in the synagogue and Jeremiah preached to the men in the street (*Pesikta Rabbati* 26:129).

4. When King Josiah restored the worship of God, Jeremiah brought back the ten exiled tribes (Talmud, *Arachin* 33a).

5. The fourth chapter of the Book of Lamentations, traditionally ascribed to Jeremiah, begins with a dirge for Josiah (*Lamentations Rabbah* 1:18).

6. Jeremiah was commanded by God to go to Anathoth because his merits were so great that God could not destroy Jerusalem as long as Jeremiah was in the city. In Jeremiah's absence, Jerusalem was conquered and the city set on fire. When Jeremiah returned, he saw smoke rising from the Temple. He rejoiced, thinking that the Jews had repented and that the smoke was that of the sacrifice to make amends. He wept bitterly when he realized his error (*Peskita Rabbati* 26:131).

7. The sages taught that Jeremiah wrote not only his own book, but the Books of Kings and Lamentations as well (Talmud, *Bava Batra* 15a).

Notable Quotations

1. Before I formed you in the belly I knew you, and before you came forth out of the womb I sanctified you; I have appointed you a prophet unto the nations (Jeremiah 1:5).

2. Go and cry in the ears of Jerusalem, saying: Thus says God: I remember for you the affection of your youth, the love of your espousals. How you went after Me in the wilderness, in a land that was not sown (Jeremiah 2:1).

3. To what purpose is to Me the frankincense that comes from Sheba, and the sweet cane from a far country? Your burnt offerings are not acceptable, nor your sacrifices pleasing to Me (Jeremiah 6:20).

4. Then will I cause to cease from the cities of Judah, and from the streets of Jerusalem, the voice of mirth and gladness, the voice of the bridegroom and the voice of the bride . . . (Jeremiah 7:34). [Note: A part of this verse is used as the last of the seven wedding blessings in a traditional Jewish wedding ceremony.]

5. Is there no balm in Gilead? Is there no physician there? Why then is not the health of the daughter of my people recovered? (Jeremiah 8:22).

6. Pour out your wrath upon the nations, that do not know You, and upon the families that call not on Your name . . . (Jeremiah 10:25).

7. Can the Ethiopian change his skin, or the leopard his spots? Then may you also do good, that are accustomed to do evil (Jeremiah 13:23).

8. Why is my pain perpetual, and my wound incurable, so that it refuses to be healed? Will You indeed be unto me as a deceitful brook, as waters that fail? (Jeremiah 15:18).

9. Behold, I will cause to cease out of this place, before your eyes and in your days, the voice of mirth and the voice of gladness, the voice of the

bridegroom and the voice of the bride (Jeremiah 15:9).

10. Blessed is the man that trusts in God, and whose trust the Lord is. For he shall be as a tree planted by the waters, and that spreads out its roots by the river. And shall not see when heat comes, but its foliage shall be luxuriant . . . (Jeremiah 17:8).

11. Behold, the days come, says God, that I will raise unto David a righteous shoot, and he shall reign as king and prosper, and shall execute justice and righteousness in the land (Jeremiah 23:5).

12. Thus says God: The people that were left of the sword have found grace in the wilderness, even Israel, when I go to cause him to rest (Jeremiah 31:1).

13. Thus says God: A voice is heard in Ramah, lamentation and bitter weeping, Rachel weeping for her children. She refuses to be comforted for her children, because they are gone (Jeremiah 31:14).

14. Is Ephraim a darling son to Me? Is he a child that is dandled? For as often as I speak of him, I do earnestly remember him still. Therefore my heart yearns for him and I will surely have compassion upon him, says God (Jeremiah 31:19).

15. In those days they shall say no more: "The fathers have eaten sour grapes, and the children's

teeth are set on edge." But every one shall die for his own iniquity; every man that eats the sour grapes, his teeth shall be set on edge (Jeremiah 31:28–29).

Ezekiel

Ezekiel and His Family

The name Ezekiel—in Hebrew, *Yehezkel*—seems to be derived from the Hebrew *yechezak El*, meaning "may God strengthen." He was a priest, the son of Buzi, born of the priestly family of Zadok, and was married to a woman who suddenly died during the siege of Jerusalem (Ezekiel 24:15). Ezekiel, the third of the three Major Prophets, is said to have begun prophesying in the fifth year of Jehoiachin's exile in Babylonia, seven years before the final fall of the holy city of Jerusalem. He lived during the last days of the First Temple and received inspiration from the prophetic utterances of Jeremiah, his elder contemporary.

Ezekiel was carried away captive by the Babylonians from the Holy Land with King Jehoiachin, living in Tel-Aviv on the banks of the Chebar River. He received his prophetic call five years after he had arrived in Babylon, but there is no indication given of the length of his tenure as prophet. There is also no authentic record of the date of his death or the place where he was buried. There is, however, a tradition that asserts that he died in Babylon during the reign of King Nebuchadnezzar and was buried at Kefil between the Euphrates and Chebar Rivers.

Place in the Canon

The talmudic arrangement of the three Major Prophets is Jeremiah, Ezekiel, and Isaiah. This departure from the true historical order (Isaiah, Jeremiah, and Ezekiel) is justified, according to the talmudic tractate of *Bava Batra* 14b, which asserts: "The Book of Kings ends with doom, Jeremiah is all doom. Ezekiel begins with doom but ends with consolation, while Isaiah is all consolation, so we place doom alongside doom and consolation alongside consolation."

Subject Matter and Book Summary

The Book of Ezekiel is forty-eight chapters in length. The first twenty-four chapters are, on the whole, prophecies of doom and destruction, while the latter twenty-four chapters are prophecies of consolation.

Ezekiel's call to prophecy took place in the fifth year of King Jehoiachin's captivity (593–592 B.C.E.).

In the opening chapter of the book, Ezekiel has one of the most remarkable of all visions. It is the vision of the Divine Throne-Chariot, a strange and mysterious apparition whose main feature was its ability to be drawn by four-faced living creatures. In the vision of the departing Throne-Chariot, Ezekiel read the impending departure of the Divine Presence from the Temple in Jerusalem and the fall of Judea.

In chapter 2, God speaks to Ezekiel: "Son of man, stand upon your feet, and I will speak with you." The phrase "son of man" occurs frequently in the Book of Ezekiel and is likely intended to emphasize that although he was privileged to witness the majestic heavenly vision of the Throne-Chariot, he was nevertheless nothing more than a human being. Awestruck by the majestic sight of the Divine glory, Ezekiel falls upon his face. When God sets him straight up on his feet, Ezekiel's ministry officially commences.

The following is a synopsis of the events in the Book of Ezekiel, chapter by chapter:

1:1–31–3:21	The revelation to Ezekiel and his call to prophecy
3:22–24:27	The prophecies concerning the destruction of Judah and Jerusalem
3:22–5:17	House arrest and symbol of siege of Jerusalem
6:1–7:27	Prophecies against the mountains of Israel
8:1–11:25	The spirit of God transports Ezekiel from Babylon to Jerusalem

CHAPTER 25—1–32:32

CHAPTERS 40:1–48:35—
A MESSIANIC PRIESTLY CODE

Ezekiel's Style

More than any other prophet, Ezekiel makes vivid use of graphic imagery, symbol, and parable to illustrate his message. Perhaps the most remarkable section of his book is the opening chapter, in which he envisions God's Chariot, drawn by four-faced living creatures with wings and wheels for mobility. The rabbinic attempt to understand and interpret this opening vision gave rise to a system of esoteric thought known as *Ma'aseh Merkavah* (happenings of the Divine Chariot), around which Jewish mysticism and its studies centered. Another famous vision appears in chapter 37, a metaphor for the revival of the Jewish people. According to

Ezekiel, God sets him down in a valley filled with lifeless bones. The bones have been in the hot sun for such a long period of time that the skin has been stripped from them. God then asks Ezekiel: "O son of man, can these bones live again?" "Only You know," Ezekiel replies, whereupon God orders him to prophesy to the bones: "O dry bones, hear the word of God. I will cause breath to enter into you and you shall live again." The bones begin coming together, flesh grows upon them, and soon the bones form into bodies. God then fills the bones with breath, and the corpses proceed to rise on their feet. Then Ezekiel proclaims: "O mortal, these bones are the whole House of Israel."

Also striking in the Book of Ezekiel are the numerous symbolic actions by which the prophet illustrates his orations. For instance, in chapters 4 and 5 of the book, Ezekiel describes the siege, capture, and destruction of the holy city of Jerusalem. As chapter 5 begins, Ezekiel indicates the nation of Israel's fate with the symbolic act of a sharp sword:

> And you, son of man, take a sharp sword, as a barber's razor shall you take it, and cause it to pass upon your head and upon your beard. Then take the balances to weigh, and divide the hair. A third part shall you burn in the first in the midst of the city, when the days of the siege are fulfilled. You shall take a third part and smite it with the sword round about her. And a third part you shall scatter to the wind, and I will draw out a sword after them. You shall take a few by number, and bind them in your skirts. And of them you shall take again, and

cast them into the midst of the fire, and burn them in the fire. Therefrom shall a fire come forth unto all of the house of Israel. (Ezekiel 5:1–4)

At the conclusion of this symbolic act, God explains that the act indicates the impending destruction of the people by massacre and dispersion.

In most instances, Ezekiel actually performs the symbolic actions. As one of the first persons to introduce symbolism into Hebrew literature, Ezekiel has been called the "father of apocalypse."

Ezekiel in Rabbinic Legend and Writings

Four aspects of Ezekiel's prophetic career figure to the greatest degree in rabbinic literature: the Divine Chariot (chapter 1), which became the basis of Jewish mysticism; the harsh denunciations of Israel, which were somewhat unacceptable to the rabbis because of the fact that they might be exploited by the church for anti-Jewish, polemical reasons; the resurrection of the dry bones, which was downplayed by some rabbis because it was a potentially popular theme for sectarian deliberation; and Ezekiel's vision of a future Temple, which appears to contradict some of the rules in the Five Books of Moses.

The following are some rabbinic citations related to the Book of Ezekiel that will help to summarize the way in which the rabbis viewed the prophet and his ideas:

1. The Talmud reveals the fact that at one time the Book of Ezekiel was in danger of not being included in the scriptural canon. Note this talmudic reference from the tractate *Shabbat* 13b: "Rav Judah said, in the name of Rav: In truth that man is to be remembered for blessing. His name is Chananiah son of Hezekiah. Had it not been for him, the Book of Ezekiel would have been withdrawn, because its teachings seem to contradict those of the Torah."

2. According to the *Midrash* (*Genesis Rabbah* 5:5), God commanded the heavens to open before Ezekiel, perhaps as a counterweight to similar claims on behalf of Jesus—according to Rabbi Eliezer, "a maidservant saw at the Red Sea what Ezekiel and all the other prophets never saw" (*Mechilta, Shirah* 3).

3. In line with his nationalistic tendency, Rabbi Eliezer prohibited the *Haftarah* reading (chapter 16 of the Book of Ezekiel), which describes Jerusalem's abominations.

4. Rabbi Eliezer reduced the significance of Ezekiel's vision of the dry bones, stating that "the dead whom Ezekiel revived stood up, recited a song of praise, and immediately died" (Talmud, *Sanhedrin* 92b).

5. Ezekiel is praised for his love of Israel, and thus he was deemed worthy to perform the resuscitation miracle (*Seder Eliyah Rabbah* 5:23). He was criticized, however, for his doubting of the possibility of such a miracle, and because of his lack of

faith and trust, he was punished by being brought to death on foreign soil (*Pirke de Rabbi Eliezer* 33).

6. Like Jeremiah, Ezekiel, too, was said to have been a descendant of Joshua by his marriage with the proselyte Rahab (Talmud, *Megillah* 14b).

7. Rabbinically speaking, Ezekiel's greatest miracle was his resuscitation of the dead, which is recounted in Ezekiel 37. There are different rabbinic traditions as to the fate of these people, both before and after their resurrection. Some say they were godless people, who in their lifetime had denied the resurrection. Others posited that they were Ephraimites who tried to escape from Egypt before Moses and perished in the attempt. There are still others who maintain that after King Nebuchadnezzar had carried the youths of Judah to Babylon, he had them executed because their beauty had entranced the Babylonian women. It was these youths, according to some opinions, that Ezekiel called back to life. The miracle was performed on the same day on which the three men were cast into the fiery furnace, namely, on the Sabbath and on the Day of Atonement (*Song of Songs Rabbah* 7:9).

Major Concepts and Teachings

1. Individual Responsibility: Ezekiel dealt with the problem of individual responsibility and moral freedom. His fellow exiles, who considered themselves better than their fathers, complained that

they were being punished for the sins of their ancestors. Ezekiel asserted that the acts of past generations neither determine the response of the present generation nor shape their future. Each individual person is to be judged on the basis of what he or she does, and all individuals are responsible for their own destinies. Here is Ezekiel in his own words:

> The word of God came to me: What do you mean by quoting this proverb upon the soil of Israel, "Fathers eat sour grapes and their children's teeth are blunted"? As I live, declares the Lord God, this proverb shall no longer be current among you in Israel. Consider, all lives are Mine; the life of the father and the life of the son are both Mine. The person who sins, only he shall die. (Ezekiel 18:1–4)

2. Holiness: The fundamental principle of Ezekiel's vision of the future Temple is holiness: "And they (i.e., the priests) shall teach My people the difference between the holy and the common, and cause them to discern between the unclean and the clean." The correct understanding of the term "holiness" sheds light on the regulations concerning the structure of the restored Temple and its ritual, which are aimed at separating that which is holy from that which is common and mundane.

3. Repentance: Ezekiel in his book introduces the idea of repentance—in Hebrew, *teshuvah*. It is one of Judaism's most important concepts and suggests that no person is condemned by the past nor should be judged by it. Moreover, even if a person has

done wrong, people have the capacity to choose freely in order to change their ways. God is eager to accept a person's penitence. Here are several verses from Ezekiel to illustrate this teaching:

> Is it my desire that a wicked man shall die? says God. It is rather that he shall turn back from his ways and live. (Ezekiel 18:23)

> Cast away all the transgressions by which you have offended, and get yourselves a new heart and a new spirit, that you may not die, O House of Israel. For it is not My desire that anyone shall die—declares the Lord God. Repent, therefore, and live. (Ezekiel 18:31–32)

4. Israel's Restoration: Like the prophets before him, Ezekiel predicted not only the return of the Babylonian exile and the rebuilding of the Jerusalem Temple, but also the ultimate redemption of Israel in the distant future. Many of Ezekiel's Messianic prophecies resemble those of Isaiah. For example, the verse in Ezekiel 34:25 "I will make with them a covenant of peace, and will cause evil beasts to cease out of the land; and they shall dwell safely in the wilderness, and sleep in the woods" is reminiscent of Isaiah's Messianic vision that "the wolf shall dwell with the lamb . . ." (Isaiah 11:6). One major difference between the prophecy of Ezekiel and that of Isaiah is the fact that Isaiah referred to a change in the natural instincts of the wild beast and universal peace for humankind, whereas Ezekiel simply predicted the banishment of beasts of prey and is concerned only with the future people of Israel.

Notable Quotations

1. And I looked up, and behold, a stormy wind came out of the north, a great cloud, with a fire flashing up, so that a brightness was round about it; and out of the midst thereof as the color of electrum, out of the midst of the fire (Ezekiel 1:4).

2. And God said to me: "Son of man, stand up upon your feet, and I will speak with you." And spirit entered into me when God spoke to me, and set me upon my feet; and I heard Him that spoke to me (Ezekiel 2:1–2).

3. Then a spirit lifted me up, and I heard behind me the voice of great rushing: "Blessed be the glory of God from His place" (Ezekiel 3:12).

4. And I will give them one heart, and I will put a new spirit within you; and I will remove the stony heart out of their flesh, and will give them a heart of flesh (Ezekiel 11:19).

5. And the word of God came to me saying: "What do you mean that you use this proverb in the land of Israel, saying: The fathers have eaten sour grapes, and the children's teeth are set on edge?" (Ezekiel 18:1–2).

6. And I will put hooks in your jaws, and I will cause the fish of your rivers to stick to your scales; and I will bring you up out of the midst of your

rivers, and all the fish of your rivers shall stick to your scales (Ezekiel 29:4).

7. And I will sprinkle clean water upon you, and you shall be clean; from all your uncleannesses and from all your idols, will I cleanse you (Ezekiel 36:25).

8. And He said to me: "Son of man, can these bones live?" And I answered: "O God, You know" (Ezekiel 37:3).

9. Thus says the Lord God: No alien, uncircumcised in heart and uncircumcised in flesh, shall enter into My sanctuary, even any alien that is among the children of Israel (Ezekiel 44:9).

10. And they shall teach My people the difference between the holy and the common, and cause them to discern between the unclean and the clean (Ezekiel 44:23).

11. And by the river upon the bank thereof, on this side and on that side, shall grow every tree for food, whose leaf shall not wither, neither shall the fruit thereof fail; it shall bring forth new fruit every month, because the waters thereof issue out of the sanctuary; and the fruit thereof shall be for food, and the leaf thereof for healing (Ezekiel 47:12).

14

The Twelve Minor Prophets

Hosea

Composition and Authorship

The Book of Hosea occupies the first place among the so-called twelve Minor Prophets. The name "Minor Prophets," as compared with "Major Prophets" (Isaiah, Jeremiah, and Ezekiel), does not refer to value but to volume—the length of the individual books. Since each of these twelve books was very short, they were gathered into a single collection to safeguard their preservation. For this reason, they count as one book in the Hebrew Bible and are commonly known as "The Twelve."

Chronologically, the Book of Hosea is after the Book of Amos, but it is placed first because of its length. Hosea, the Prophet, lived after Amos during the eighth century before the Common Era and prophesied in the Kingdom of Israel before Isaiah did in the Kingdom of Judah. Hosea's prophetic work began before the death of King Jeroboam II, and he was still living when the kingdom of Israel was destroyed by the Assyrians in 721 B.C.E.

Most of Hosea's prophecies are oracles of doom. The people of Israel had forsaken God's covenant by worshiping foreign deities. Lack of trust in God led the Israelites to seek help from neighboring nations, which in turn increased Israel's immorality. For this, God would punish the people and send them into exile. However, in spite of all of this, God will again purify the people because His bond of love for them is everlasting.

Subject Matter and Contents

Hosea's fourteen-chapter book falls into two main divisions. Chapters 1–3 are largely autobiographical, explaining how Hosea become a prophet. God orders Hosea to take for himself a wife of harlotry. This he does, marrying Gomer, who later becomes unfaithful to him. According to some biblical commentators, the Hosea narrative is an allegorical parable describing God's love for Israel in terms of the prophet's tragic love for the allegedly faithless Gomer. Israel's faithlessness to God is the principal theme of Hosea's prophecy, predicting their dire punishment and ultimate deliverance through sincere repentance.

The following is a synopsis of the major events in the Book of Hosea:

1:1–9	Hosea's marriage to Gomer, and the birth of their children Jezreel and Lo-ruchamah.
2:1–3	Promise of redemption

2:4–15	Israel's infidelity
2:16–25	Israel's redemption
3:1–3	Hosea is commanded to take his erring wife back
4:1–19	Israel is arraigned by God
5:1–7	Denunciation of priests and rules
5:8–15	Description of the coming punishment
6:–7:2	The people's corruption
7:3–7	National depravity
7:8–16	Israel's political maneuvers
8:1–3	Alarm of war
8:4–14	Doom of the nation and its false gods
9:1–9	Israel's anguish in exile
9:10–17	Israel's corruption
10:1–8	Israel's misused prosperity
10:9–15	The harvest of Israel's idolatry
11:1–11	God's paternal love for Israel
12:1–15	Israel's backsliding
13:1–15	Judgment upon Israel
14:1–10	Final call to repentance

Hosea in Rabbinic Writings

The following is a cross-section of citations from rabbinic literature related to Hosea and his book.

1. Hosea is spoken of as the greatest of his prophetical contemporaries (Talmud, *Pesachim* 87a).

2. Hosea's father, Beeri, was believed to have been a prophet and his prophecy incorporated into Isaiah 8:19 (*Leviticus Rabbah* 6:6 and 15:2).

3. Not all of Hosea's prophecies are arranged in chronological order, just as the books of the Bible themselves are not in chronological order (Talmud, *Bava Batra* 14a).

4. Hosea prophesied concerning Israel for ninety years (*Pirke de Rabbi Eliezer* 33:90).

5. Hosea was the first prophet to proclaim the greatness of repentance, teaching that it reaches the Throne of Glory (Hosea 14:2). His ancestor Reuben was rewarded for having repented of his hostile behavior toward Joseph (*Genesis Rabbah* 84:19).

6. According to one opinion, the rabbinic concept of the "merits of the fathers" (which implies that the good deeds of the ancestors contribute to the welfare of their descendants) ceased in Hosea's lifetime.

Major Concepts and Teachings

1. Ethical Monotheism: According to Hosea, God's demand was not sacrifice and ritual but a piety and spirituality that expressed itself in love and loyalty. Like Amos, Hosea elevated the Israelite religion by emphasizing the moral and ethical aspects of religiosity.

2. God and Israel's love relationship is that of husband and wife: Hosea is the first prophet to

employ the husband-and-wife allegory. Whereas Amos thinks of God in terms of King and Judge, Hosea delineates God under the imagery of a compassionate husband. Two noteworthy verses in chapter 22 carry the Jew back to the revelation on Sinai when God effected a "spiritual marriage" with Israel, with the Torah as dowry. These two verses are recited when phylacteries (*tefillin*) are donned:

> And I will betroth you to Me forever
> I will betroth you to Me in righteousness and
>   justice,
> And in lovingkindness and in compassion,
> And I will betroth you unto Me in faithfulness
> And you shall know the Lord. (Hosea 2:21–22)

3. Faithlessness begets sin: Hosea's prophecies are emphatic in their denunciation of the Israelites and their rulers who sunk to the depths of corruption. Hosea considers infidelity to be the chief sin, of which Israel, the adulterous wife, has been guilty against her loving husband, God. Hosea asserts emphatically that such behavior would be punished through suffering in Israel. There, the people would be purged and purified and allowed to return to God. In the words of the Book of Hosea: "I will heal their backsliding, and I will love them freely. For My anger is turned away from him" (Hosea 14:5).

Notable Quotations

1. When the Lord spoke at first with Hosea, the Lord said to him: "Go and take for yourself a wife of harlotry and children of harlotry; for the land does commit great harlotry, departing from the Lord" (Hosea 1:2).

2. And I will betroth you to Me forever; yea, I will betroth you unto Me in righteousness and in justice; and in lovingkindness and in compassion. And I will betroth you to Me in faithfulness, and you shall know the Lord (Hosea 2:21–22).

3. Come and let us return to God; for He has torn, and he will heal us; he has smitten, and He will bind us (Hosea 6:1).

4. They shall walk after God, who shall roar like a lion; and the children shall come trembling from the west (Hosea 12:10).

5. Return, O Israel, unto the Lord your God, for you have stumbled in your iniquity (Hosea 14:2).

6. I will heal their backsliding, and I will love them freely; for My anger is turned away from him. I will be as the dew unto Israel; he shall blossom as the lily and cast forth his roots as Lebanon (Hosea 14:5–6).

Joel

Composition and Authorship

The name "Joel" means the "Lord is God." The Book of Joel, four chapters in length, is the second book in the Minor Prophets, and the book's superscription names the Prophet Joel, son of Pethuel, as the author. Nothing is known of the author's life, time, place, or residence. Even the date of the book is subject to speculation and is widely disputed among Bible scholars. There are no references to kings, princes, or national leaders—only to priests and elders. Joel is placed either in a very early period (i.e., before 800 B.C.E.) or in post-exilic times (after 500 B.C.E.). The reason for these dates is that there is no mention of Assyria, which did not emerge as a power before 760 B.C.E., nor is there any reference to Babylon, which had fallen by 537 B.C.E.

The style of the book is fluent, clear, and of a high order. Its general subject is Divine judgment.

Subject Matter and Contents of Book

The book begins with a graphic description of an invasion of locusts sent by God as a punishment on the nation. This plague of locusts, accompanied by a drought of unusual severity, sweeps in successive swarms over Judea and destroys the produce of the fields and vineyards. Remarkably vivid is the description of the locust swarms filling the entire air. Their destructiveness is compared to that of a mighty army:

> That which the palmer-worm has left has the locust eaten; and that which the locust has left the canker-worm has eaten; and that which the canker-worm has left has the caterpillar eaten. (Joel 1:4)

> The appearance of them is as the appearance of horses; and as horsemen, so do they run. Like the noise of chariots, on the tops of the mountains do they leap, like the noise of a flame of fire that devours the stubble, as a mighty people set in battle array. (Joel 2:4–5)

It is not known whether the plague of locusts is to be understood literally or figuratively. The early Church Fathers saw in the locusts a symbol of the lusts that attack sinful man or of the enemies that attacked Judea in their turn. Other commentators assert that the four species of locusts mentioned in the book symbolize the four invasions Judea would undergo at the hands of her enemies.

The following is a summary of the major events in the Book of Joel:

1:1–7	The plague of locusts
1:8–12	A call to mourning
1:13–20	A plea for repentance
2:1–11	The invasion of the locusts
2:12–17	The call to repentance
2:18–27	God's response
2:28–32	The holy spirit of prophecy will be bestowed upon both young and old
3:1–3	God's assize
3:4–8	Indictment of Tyre, Zidon, and Philistia
3:9–17	God's day of retribution
3:18–21	God's award

Major Concepts and Teachings

1. God is merciful and accepts those who seek penitence: Joel exhorts the priests, the elders, and all the people to seek God's mercy through repentance, fasting, and prayer. He promises that God will have pity on His people, bringing an end to the plague and a time of fruitfulness and peace. Here is the concept in the prophet's own words: "Yet even now, says God, turn to Me with all your heart, and with fasting, weeping and lamentation. Rend your heart, and not your garments, and turn to the Lord your God; For God is gracious and compassionate, long suffering and abounding in mercy, and renouncing punishment" (Joel 2:12–13).

2. There will be a Day of Judgment when the nations that behaved cruelly toward the people of

Israel will be punished: Chapter 4 of the Book of Joel depicts the Day of Judgment in the valley of Jehoshaphat, foretelling the punishment that will be accorded to the nations that sold Israel into slavery.

3. God's abode is in Jerusalem, the holy city: Joel reiterates the fact that when God chooses to make Jerusalem His abode, then Jerusalem takes on the status of a holy city. Joel's final word in his book is that "God dwells in Zion" (Joel 4:21).

Notable Quotations

1. Blow the horn in Zion, and sound an alarm in My holy mountain; let all the inhabitants of the land tremble; for the day of the Lord comes, for it is at hand (Joel 2:1).

2. They leap upon the city, and run upon the wall; they climb up into the houses and enter in at the windows like a thief (Joel 2:9).

3. . . . And your sons and your daughters shall prophesy; your old men shall dream dreams, and your youth shall see visions (Joel 3:1).

4. And I will show wonders in the heavens and in the earth; blood, and fire, and pillars of smoke (Joel 3:2). [The approaching Day of Judgment will be heralded by these three plagues, mentioned also in the Passover *Haggadah*.]

5. Beat your plowshares into swords, and your pruning hooks into spears; let the weak say: "I am strong" (Joel 4:10). [Note: This verse is a reversal of the Messianic prophecies of Isaiah 2:4, in which he states "and they shall beat their swords into plowshares, and their spears into pruning hooks."]

Amos

Composition and Authorship

Amos is the third of the Minor Prophets, according to the Hebrew Bible (between Joel and Obadiah). This eighth-century prophet, an older contemporary of Hosea, is considered the earliest of the Latter Prophets and by some is considered the first of the literary prophets (i.e., prophets whose writings are preserved in books called by their names).

Amos was a herdsman from Tekoa, a town twelve miles from Jerusalem. He lived during a prosperous era for both the Kingdoms of Judah and Israel. Syria had been defeated in war and Assyria was ruled by a series of ineffective kings. With prosperity in the Northern Kingdom of Israel came a wealthy class of Israelites who turn their backs on the poor. It is this group to which Amos turns his attention, upset that they are scrupulous about observing Temple rituals but negligent in the arena of social action. Appearing one holiday morning at the Temple of the Israelite Kingdom in Beth El, and in the presence of both the wealthy and the priests, Amos proclaims in God's name:

> I loathe, I hate your festivals,
> I am not appeased by your solemn assemblies.
> If you offer Me burnt offerings or your meal
>   offerings
> I will not accept them
> I will pay no attention to your gifts of fatlings.
>   (Amos 5:21–22)

Amos even became very sarcastic in his denunciation of ritual:

> Come to Beth El and transgress,
> To Gilgal and transgress even more
> Present your sacrifices the next morning
> And your tithes on the third day;
> And burn a thanksgiving offering of leavened
>   bread;
> And proclaim freewill offerings loudly.
> For you love that sort of thing, O Israelites,
>   declares my Lord God. (Amos 4:4–5)

According to Amos, only one thing will appease God: "Let justice well up like water, righteousness like a mighty stream" (Amos 5:24). Amos would likely have agreed with those today who criticize organized religion for ignoring the social ills of their communities.

Amos also denounces the brutalities and cruel wrongs perpetrated by various nations. He strongly insists upon social justice, respect for the lowly, and the defense of the weak against the powerful.

He condemns self-indulgence, which breeds cruelty, and compares the pampered women of Samaria to cows grown fat through feeding in the rich pastures of Bashan, east of Jordan. When the idolatrous priest of Beth El tells Amos to go back home and prophesy there, he replies that he is not a professional prophet who tries to please people but simply a shepherd who has been charged to prophesy to the people of Israel.

Tradition has differing opinions as to how Amos met his end. One source claims that he was killed by Uzziah, who struck him in the forehead with a glowing iron, while another says that he was killed by a blow on the temple struck by Amaziah, the priest of Beth El.

Amos's Style

The writings of Amos are very graphic, filled with similes and metaphors drawn from nature. Amos was also very fond of word play, as can be seen from chapter 8:2, in which God says: "Amos, what do you see?" And Amos answers: "A basket of summer fruit" [in Hebrew, *kloov kayitz*]. To which God responds: "The end [in Hebrew, *kaytz*, a play on the word *kayitz* in the previous sentence] is come upon My people Israel."

Amos also uses many words in his book that are not found elsewhere in the Bible (e.g., in 5:11, *boashashchem*, meaning "to trample").

Subject Matter and Contents

The Book of Amos falls into three divisions. Chapters 1 and 2 serve as a prologue to Amos's thesis: just as the other nations courted disaster by violating the laws of righteousness, so, too, Israel will not escape. Chapters 3 through 6 expand the charge against the people who looked upon their prosperity as evidence of their good behavior toward others. The last three chapters describe the visions that God had shown to Amos, foretelling earthquake, famine, and locusts, which remind the people that they must return to God before it is too late. The book concludes with a description of an age of peace to come.

Here is a summary of the major events in the Book of Amos:

1:1–5	Judgment on Syria
1:6–8	Judgment on Philistia
1:9–10	Judgment on Tyre
1:11–12	Judgment on Edom
1:13–15	Judgment on Ammon
2:1–3	Judgment on Moab
2:4–5	Judgment on Judah
2:6–16	Indictment of Israel
3:1–8	Approaching doom
3:9–4:3	Denouncement of Samarian women
3:4–13	Religion of the nation is denounced
5:1–3	Dirge over Israel
5:4–17	Condemnation and a call to repentance

5:18–27	The Day of the Lord
6:1–14	Impending doom
7:1–3	First Vision: Plague of Locusts
7:4–6	Second Vision: Destructive Fire
7:7–9	Third Vision: The Wall and Plumbline
7:10–17	Amos and Amaziah
8:1–3	Fourth Vision: The End of Israel
8:4–14	The coming judgment
9:1–4	The Fifth Vision: God's Sentence on Israel
9:7–15	Final message of hope

Amos in Rabbinic Writings

1. According the rabbis, Amos was nicknamed "the stutterer" by a popular etymology. The Israelites, upon hearing his bitter rebukes, retorted: "Has God cast aside all His creatures to let His spirit dwell only on this stutterer?" (*Leviticus Rabbah* 10).

2. According to rabbinic tradition, Amos was killed by King Uzziah, who struck him on the forehead with a glowing iron (*Seder HaDorot*).

3. Six hundred and thirteen commandments were given to Moses. Amos reduced them to one: "Seek Me and Live!" (Talmud, *Makkot* 24a).

Major Concepts and Teachings

1. Ritual is only a means to an end: Amos protested the sacrificial ritual that was offered by the wealthy in the Temple, since the wealthy continued to be indifferent to the poor and the weak. The point he was making in his book was that sacrifice could not be a substitute for doing justice, being honest, or showing kindness and mercy. The purpose of true sacrifice was to help people to focus more clearly on God's ethical demands.

2. Being the Chosen People does not guarantee favored treatment: Amos warns the Israelites not to expect favored treatment from God just because they are God's special people. On the contrary, Amos reminds the people that chosenness implies and imposes further obligations on them, not simply rights: "You alone have I singled out of all the families of the earth. That is why I call you to account for all of your sins" (Amos 3:2).

3. Righteousness is the basis of both national and individual life: The master-word of existence to Amos is "righteousness," which to him, as to his successors, means holiness of life in the individual and the triumph of justice in the world. For Amos, God Himself is righteousness, being that He is the God of all families of the earth, judging them alike according to their humane dealings toward their fellow human beings. Man's inhumanity to man, is, according to Amos, the cardinal sin.

4. God is the Father of all of humanity. Amos affirms that the Lord of the universe has concern for all of his creatures. This idea is expressed forcefully in the following passage: "To Me, O Israelites, you are just like the Ethiopians, declares God. True, I brought Israel up from the land of Egypt, but also the Philistines from Caphtor and the Arameans from Kir" (Amos 9:7).

Here, Amos says that the Jews are no closer to God than the inhabitants of the farthermost edge of the then civilized world—the Ethiopians. He makes reference to the Exodus from Egypt, the proudest moment of Jewish history, and asserts that God had done as much for their worst enemy—the Philistines. In the view of Amos, God is not simply the Creator of the world but the Father of humanity.

Notable Quotations

1. Thus says God: For three transgressions of Damascus, yea for four, I will not reverse it: because they have threshed Gilead with sledges of iron (Amos 1:3).

2. . . . Because they sell the righteous for silver, and the needy for a pair of hoes. They pant after the dust of the earth on the head of the poor, and turn aside the way of the humble; and a man and his father to the same maid, to profane My holy name (Amos 2:6–7).

3. You only have I known of all the families of the earth; therefore, will I visit upon you all your transgressions (Amos 3:2).

4. Will two walk together, except they have agreed? Will a lion roar in the forest when he has no prey . . . ? (Amos 3:3-4).

5. Hate the evil and love the good, and establish justice in the gate . . . (Amos 5:15).

6. I hate, I despise your feasts, and I will take no delight in your solemn assemblies (Amos 5:21).

7. Let justice well up as waters, and righteousness as a mighty stream (Amos 5:24).

8. Are you not as the children of the Ethiopians to Me, O children of Israel? says God . . . (Amos 9:7).

Obadiah

Composition and Authorship

Obadiah (Hebrew for "servant of God") is the author of the shortest book in the Bible. This single-chapter book is the fourth of the Books of the Minor Prophets. Nothing is known of this prophet, and there is wide disagreement regarding the time in which his book was composed. In the Talmud (*Sanhedrin* 39b) the rabbis identified Obadiah with the one who lived in King Ahab's reign (1 Kings 18:3), and they considered him an Edomite proselyte descended from Eliphaz, son of Esau (*Yalkut Shimoni*, Obadiah). Other views place him as early as 889 B.C.E. and as late as 312 B.C.E., with many advocates of dates inbetween. The question of date is complicated by the fact that there is a striking resemblance between passages in the Book of Obadiah and those in Jeremiah. Verses 1–4 and 5–6 are somewhat similar to those of Jeremiah 49:14–16 and 9–10, so that it is assumed that one quotes from the other or both used a common source.

154

Subject Matter

In his book, Obadiah predicts the destruction of Edom, representing the forces of evil. He severely condemns the Edomites for having refused to assist Jerusalem in the day of calamity and expresses the conviction that they will be treated measure for measure, for they helped the Babylonians to bring about the downfall of Judea. From their mountainous strongholds, south of the Dead Sea, the warlike Edomites, archenemies of the Jews, looked down upon their neighbors in Jerusalem.

Obadiah's prophecy is reminiscent of Psalms 137, containing an outburst of hatred against the enemies of Jerusalem who rejoiced at its fall: "Remember, O God, against the Edomites the day of Jerusalem, when they said: Raze it, raze it, down to its foundation" (Psalms 137:7).

The confidence that Edom shall not ultimately triumph over Israel has today become an expression of a spiritual conviction of permanent value that Judaism cannot be extinguished by the forces of evil.

Here is a summary of the events in the Book of Obadiah:

1:1–5	Prophecy of Edom's downfall
1:6–7	The downfall of Edom
1:8–9	Final destruction of Edom
1:10–14	The reason for Edom's punishment

Major Teaching in the Book

The Book of Obadiah denounces the unbrotherly and cruel conduct of the Edomites in the day of Israel's ruin, when Jerusalem was destroyed by the Babylonians. Other nations in later times have played the cruel role of Edom and manifested wanton hatred toward Israel. Obadiah predicts triumph over them all. Thus, the lasting message of his book is that God can and will always break the shackles of evil. And Edom, because of its close blood relationship with Israel, continues to represent the evil oppressor and persecutor of the people of Israel.

Notable Quotations

1. Though you make your nest as high as the eagle, and though you set it among the stars, I will bring you down from there, says God (Obadiah 1:4).

2. For the day of God is near upon all the nations; as you have done, so shall it be done to you; your dealing shall return upon your own head (Obadiah 1:15).

3. And saviors shall come up on Mount Zion to judge the mount of Esau, and the kingdom shall be the Lord's (Obadiah 1:21).

Jonah

Composition and Authorship

The Book of Jonah, the fifth book of the Twelve Minor Prophets, records a prophet's experiences rather than his utterances. The Book of Jonah contains a prophecy of only one sentence—"forty days more, and Nineveh shall be overthrown" (Jonah 3:4). The book may have been added to the list of Books of the Minor Prophets because of a prophet by the name of Jonah, known from the time of the eighth-century King Jeroboam II (2 Kings 14:25) and because the book deals with the problem of a man whose mission it was to bring the word of God to the people of Nineveh.

The story of the Book of Jonah is well-known. Ordered by God to prophesy the destruction of Nineveh for its wickedness, Jonah attempted to escape from the Divine command by sailing from the Land of Israel. After his wonderful deliverance from drowning by being sheltered in the body of a big fish, he was obedient to a second commission from God. Jonah went to Nineveh and there proclaimed that it would be destroyed in forty days. God spared the city when he saw the repentance of its people. It is ironic that Jonah, a prophet who attempts to flee from his Divine mission, is the only prophet to be successful in changing the ways of a people, who are spared from destruction!

Synopsis of Book

The following is a brief summary of the major events in the Book of Jonah:

1:1–6	Jonah is commissioned by God and subsequently flees to Tarshish.
1:7–10	The sailors learn that Jonah is the cause of the storm.
1:11–16	Jonah is cast into the sea.
2:1–2	Jonah is swallowed.
2:3–10	In the fish's belly Jonah recites a Psalm of Thanksgiving.
2:11	Jonah is saved. The fish spews him forth onto dry land.
3:1–4	Jonah proceeds on his mission.
3:5–9	The people of Nineveh repent and are forgiven by God.
4:1–4	Jonah is displeased because the Ninevites have been saved.
4:5–11	Jonah is given an object lesson by God, using a plant and a worm.

Major Concepts and Teachings

1. It is impossible for a prophet to shirk his Divine mission: Although Jonah tries to escape God's will by fleeing to Tarshish, he learns that this cannot be accomplished. Even the sea and the great fish, which in mythology are independent powers in the universe, have to obey the orders of God. God orders the sea to become stormy and then calm (Jonah 1:3, 15) and the fish swallows Jonah and spews him out according to God's order (Jonah 2:1, 11). The plant and the worm at the end of the Book of Jonah are also dutiful servants to God's orders.

2. God forgives the penitent: The Book of Jonah ought certainly to be understood as a lesson in Divine forgiveness and mercy. Jonah tries to escape his mission precisely because he knows in his heart that God often does relent after having decreed punishment. The Book of Jonah is therefore designed to show that kindness of heart on the part of God and readiness to repent may be found everywhere among people, including the people of the heathen city of Nineveh.

3. God can and does answer prayer: Verses 3–10 of chapter 2 are Jonah's prayer to God while inside of the great fish: "I called out of my affliction to God, and He answered me; out of the belly of the netherworld I cried, and You heard my voice." The spirit of absolute submission to God's will that marks Jonah's prayer brings God to the realization

that Jonah has learned his lesson. Once God's purpose has been accomplished, God answers Jonah's prayer by restoring him onto dry land.

Jonah in Rabbinic Writings

1. The tribal affinities of Jonah constitute a point of controversy. Generally assigned to Asher, he is claimed for Zebulun by Rabbi Yochanan on the strength of his place of residence (2 Kings 14:24). These opinions were harmonized by the assumption that his mother was of Asher while his father was of Zebulun (Jerusalem Talmud, *Sukkah* 5:1, *Genesis Rabbah* 98:11). According to another authority, Jonah's mother was the woman of Zaraphath who entertained Elijah (*Pirke De Rabbi Eliezer* 33).

3. Jonah is said to have attained a very advanced age of more than 120 years (*Seder Olam*).

4. Jonah, the son of Zaraphath, never died. Rather, the holy spirit descended upon him while he participated in the festivities of the last day of the Festival of Sukkot (Jerusalem Talmud, *Sukkot* 5:1 and *Ecclesiastes Rabbah* 8:10).

5. When Jonah went to Jaffa, he found no ship, for the vessel on which he had intended to take passage had sailed two days before. But God caused a contrary wind to arise and the ship was driven back to port (*Zohar, Chayye Sarah*). At this Jonah rejoiced, regarding it as indicating that his plan

would succeed, and in his joy he paid his passage money in advance.

6. The storm that overtook Jonah is described as being one of the three most noteworthy storms (*Ecclesiastes Rabbah* 1:6).

7. The fish that swallowed Jonah had been created in the very beginning of the world in order to perform this work (*Zohar, Vayakhel,* and *Pirke De Rabbi Eliezer* 10).

8. The great fish died as soon as Jonah had entered into it, but was revived after three days. When Jonah was thrown into the sea his soul immediately left his body and soared up to God's throne, where it was judged and sent back. As soon as it touched the mouth of the fish on its way back to the body, the fish died but was later restored to life (*Zohar, Vayakhel*).

9. The gourd of Jonah was enormous. Before its appearance, Jonah was tortured by the heat and by a variety of insects. His clothes were burned by the heat of the belly of the great fish and he was again tortured after the storm had caused the gourd to wither. This caused Jonah to pray that God should be merciful and not a strict judge (*Pirke De Rabbi Eliezer* 10).

Modern Interpretations of the Book of Jonah

Modern scholars consider the Book of Jonah to be either a parable or an allegory. The main motifs of the book are similar to those found in the literature of other cultures. Many stories tell about a person's being swallowed by a great fish and being rescued thereafter (e.g., Heracles, the Hesione). However, only in the Book of Jonah is man rescued not by force of fire from inside or sword from outside but by prayer.

As a parable, the Book of Jonah would be an attempt to teach the lessons of repentance and prayer by means of an imaginative story. According to an allegorical interpretation, G.A. Smith, a Christian Hebraist, asserts that Jonah is representative of Israel. His disappearance in the sea symbolizes the exile, and his ejection upon dry land the restoration.

In Christianity, Jonah is regarded as proof of the capacity of Gentiles for salvation. This is the "sign of Jonas" referred to in the Book of Luke 11:29–39 in the New Testament. In the same passage he is referred to as a forerunner of Jesus.

In Islam, Yunus (Jonah), the "man of the fish," was one of the most prominent descendants of Abraham. He was one of the apostles of Allah because he thought that Allah did not control him (*Sura* 6:86).

Notable Quotations

1. . . . Come, let us cast lots, in order that we may know for whose cause this evil is upon us (Jonah 1:7).

2. And he said: I called out of my affliction, unto God, and He answered me; out of the belly of the netherworld I cried, and You heard my voice (Jonah 2:3).

3. And the people of Nineveh believed God; and they proclaimed a fast, and put on sackcloth, from the greatest of them even to the least of them (Jonah 3:5).

4. And God said: You had pity on the gourd, for which you have not labored, neither did you make it grow, which came up in a night and perished in a night. And should not I have pity on Nineveh, that great city, wherein are more than sixscore thousand persons that cannot discern between their right hand and their left, and also much cattle? (Jonah 4:10–11).

Micah

Composition and Authorship

The Book of Micah is the sixth book in the collection of the Twelve Minor Prophets within the subdivision "Later Prophets" of the second division of the Hebrew Bible (the Prophets). Although Micah's prophecies refer especially to the southern kingdom of Judah, they concern all of Israel. Micah, speaking for the people against the ruling authorities threatening them with destruction and exile, was a younger contemporary of both the Prophets Isaiah and Hosea who began their poetic careers toward the end of the eighth century before the Common Era. Both envisioned the Messianic future when war among nations would be no more.

Of the Prophet Micah, only his place and time are known. His hometown was Moreshet-gath, a village in the lowland near the Philistine border, and he prophesied during the reigns of Kings Jothan, Ahaz, and Hezekiah (739–693 B.C.E.).

Synopsis of Book

Micah received the call to prophesy against the moral and social evils of his day. The eighth century before the Common Era witnessed a time of prosperity and wealth for the Kingdoms of Israel and Judah. Wealth and prosperity brought greed and unscrupulous competition. The rich continued to wax richer, while poverty grew rampant among the less fortunate. New religious cults were introduced from Assyria and Egypt.

In his book, Micah intensely denounces the pursuit of wealth, which often led the wealthy to oppress others and shirk their social and ethical responsibility to assist those in need. He denounces the corruption of rulers and judges and attacks the mistaken conception that since Israel is God's people, it is impervious to harm and attack. Finally, he announces that the result of the corrupt society of Israelites will be defeat and the destruction of the Temple, resulting in a dispersion of the Jews into exile:

> They that build up Zion with blood, and Jerusalem with iniquity . . . yet will they lean upon God, and say: "Is not the Lord in the midst of us?" Therefore shall Zion for your sake be plowed as a field, and Jerusalem shall become heaps, and the mountain of the house as the high places of a forest. (Micah 3:10–12)

Chapters 1 through 3 consist of denunciation and sin and proclamations of approaching punishment.

Chapters 4 and 5 are a message of hope and cheer.
Chapters 6 and 7 are a combination of the previous
elements.

1:1–4	God comes forth in judgment
1:5	Corruption in Israel and Judah
1:6–7	The doom of Samaria
1:8–16	Lament over the coming doom
2:1–5	The crime and its punishment
2:6	Opposition to Micah's preaching
2:7–10	The charge is pressed home
2:11	Scorn of false prophets
2:12–13	Promise of restoration
3:1–4	Denunciation of the leaders
3:5–8	Denunciation of corrupt prophets
3:9–12	The doom of Jerusalem
4:1–8	Zion's restoration and future glory
4:9–10	Exile and restoration
4:11–14	Overthrow of Israel's enemies
5:1–5	The Messianic King
5:6–8	Israel's influence among the nations
5:9–14	Purification of Israel
6:1–8	God's controversy with Israel
6:9–16	The sin of the scant measure and charge of social injustice
7:1–6	Lament over prevailing corruption
7:7–13	Israel's contrition: confession and hope
7:14–20	Prayer and praise

The Book of Micah in Rabbinic Writings

According to one opinion, Micah was a contemporary of Isaiah (Talmud, *Pesachim* 87b). According to another, he was one of the post-exilic prophets (*Pesikta DeRav Kahana* 16:128b). In a most eloquent statement in the talmudic tractate of *Makkot* 24a, it is asserted that the verse "He has shown you, O man, what is good, and what God requires of you, but to do justly, love mercy and walk humbly with God" (Micah 6:8) is a quintessence of the 613 commandments of the Bible.

Finally, the rabbis held that Micah's prophecies were redacted and canonized by the so-called Men of the Great Assembly (Talmud, *Bava Batra* 15a).

Major Teachings and Concepts

1. One must be careful when pursuing wealth: Micah fearlessly denounces the demoralizing pursuit of wealth. Wealth and greed, as we see today in our own society, can lead to mass corruption and social evils.

2. There will be an end of days when God's purposes will be fulfilled: Although in his immediate future Micah can foresee nothing but doom and judgment, he never despairs of his people. He predicts that there will be another future, under the rule of a Messianic redeemer, when Israel's

exiles will be restored to their land and God's purposes for His people will be fulfilled.

3. Ethics and kindness are more important than ritual and sacrifice: The theology of Micah shares points in common with that of Hosea when he speaks of mercy (7:18, 20) and the love of kindness (6:8) above sacrifices:

> Who is a God like unto You, that pardons the iniquity, and passes by the transgression of the remnant of His heritage? God does not retain His anger forever, because He delights in mercy. (Micah 7:18, 20).

> Will the Lord be pleased with thousands of rams, with ten thousands of rivers of oil? . . . It has been told, O man, what is good. And what the Lord does require of you: only to do justly, love mercy, and walk humbly with your God. (Micah 6:7–8)

Notable Quotations

1. For this I will wail and howl, and I will go stripped and naked. I will make a wailing like the jackals and a mourning like the ostriches (Micah 1:8).

2. Hear I pray, you heads of Jacob, and rulers of the House of Israel. Is it not for you to know justice? Who hate the good and love the evil, and who rob their skin from off them and their flesh from off their bones (Micah 3:1–2).

3. . . . For out of Zion shall go forth the law, and the word of the Lord from Jerusalem (Micah 4:2).

4. . . . They shall beat their swords into plowshares, and their spears into pruning hooks . . . (Micah 4:3).

5. They shall sit every man under his vine and under his fig tree, and none shall make them afraid. For the mouth of God has spoken (Micah 4:4).

6. Will the Lord be pleased with thousands of rams, with ten thousands of rivers of oil? . . . (Micah 6:7).

7. It has been told, O man, what is good, and what the Lord requires of you: only to do justly, love mercy, and to walk humbly with your God (Micah 6:8).

8. Who is a God like You, that pardons iniquity, and passes by the transgression of the remnant of His heritage? He retains not His anger forever, because He delights in mercy. But God will again have compassion upon us, and will subdue our iniquities, and You will cast all their sins into the depths of the sea (Micah 7:18–19). [Note: The service in which there is the custom of symbolically casting one's sins into a running brook on the first day of Rosh Hashanah is referred to as *Tashlich* ("you will cast"), a Hebrew word borrowed from Micah 7:17 ("You will cast all their sins into the depths of the sea).]

Nachum

Composition and Authorship

Nachum (in Hebrew, "God is comforted") is seventh in the order of the Books of the Twelve Minor Prophets, consisting of three chapters in length. The book is one of the best productions of biblical literature in terms of style and sublimity of thought. His writing is powerful, emotional, and dramatic, with brilliant imagery and picturesque phrases. His thoughts are compact and terse in expression.

His breathtaking account of the destruction of Nineveh, the Assyrian capital, in the year 612 B.C.E., was likely to have been written during or immediately following this historic event. Unlike other prophets, Nachum does not allude to the sins of his people. He is entirely focused upon the doom of Nineveh and its people.

Of the prophet himself, nothing is known of the man himself other than the statement in the book's title that he was an "Elkoshite" (an Arab tradition places it north of Mosul, while others have placed it in the Galilee). His name—in Hebrew, *Nachum*—may be an abbreviation for Nechemiah ("the comforter"), and he may well have been given this name because he does not mention even once the sins of the people of Judah.

Nachum's literary activity most likely took place after the reform of King Josiah (621 B.C.E.), which would indeed account for his silence concerning the sins of his people. The stage for his prophecy is set after King Josiah had fallen in the battle of Megiddo and the Israelites under the dominion of Egypt. Asshurbanipal had come and conquered Egypt and carried off its rich treasures to Nineveh. With his death also came the decline of Assyria. When Nineveh fell (c. 608 B.C.E.), there fell with it a mighty empire. Nachum concludes his prophecy on the confident note that "all that hear the report of you clap the hands over you" (Nachum 3:19).

Subject Matter and Book Synopsis

With dramatic force Nachum depicts in his book the progress of the siege and capture of the city of Nineveh, and the joy of the Israelites at its destruction, which symbolized the downfall of wickedness. "Woe to the bloody city! It is all full of lies and rapine; the prey does not depart . . . All that hear the report of you clap the hands over you; for upon whom has not your wickedness passed continually?"

Here is a summary of the events in the three chapters of the Book of Nachum:

CHAPTER 1: INTRODUCTORY CHAPTER, DESCRIBING GOD'S PROTECTION FOR THOSE WHO TRUST IN HIM AND HIS ANGER FOR THOSE WHO PROVOKE HIM

CHAPTER 2: PROVIDES A GRAPHIC ACCOUNT OF THE CAPTURE OF THE CITY, THE FLIGHT OF THE INHABITANTS, AND THE MANY SPOILS TAKEN

CHAPTER 3: CONTINUES THE THEME OF THE DESTRUCTION OF NINEVEH, ADDING THE REASON FOR ITS FALL (I.E., IT IS BEING PUNISHED FOR ITS MANY CRIMES)

Major Themes and Concepts

1. Outrage of man's inhumanity to man: Nachum is outraged at the conduct of the people of Nineveh.

God is, according to Nachum, a God that does and will take vengeance on His adversaries. Though God is long suffering (Nachum 1:3) unto those who confide in Him, His wrath will show itself in the punishment of the arrogant enemies of His people.

2. God is a moral God: The Book of Nahum depicts God's moral government of the world. He is the Avenger of wrongdoers and the sole source of security to those who trust in Him.

Notable Quotations

1. The Lord is a jealous and avenging God; the Lord avenges and is full of wrath; the Lord takes vengeance on His adversaries and He reserves wrath for His enemies (Nachum 1:2).

2. But Nineveh has been from of old like a pool of water; yet they flee away; "stand, stand"; But none looks back (Nachum 2:9).

3. Woe to the bloody city! It is full of lies and rapine. The prey does not depart (Nachum 3:1).

4. There is no assuaging of your hurt; your wound is grievous; all that hear the report of you clap the hands over you; for upon whom has not your wickedness passed continually? (Nachum 3:19).

Habbakuk

Composition and Authorship

Habakkuk (from the Akkadian *hambaquau*, a fragrant herb) is a three-chapter book, eighth in the Books of the Minor Prophets. Nothing is known of the personal life of Habbakuk, the great prophet, who, like Job, asked searching questions and received answers from God. Based upon his message, it would appear that he prophesied shortly after the discovery by King Josiah of a Scroll of Law in the Temple in 621 B.C.E., since he makes no overt mention of the transgression of the people. Some scholars maintain that Habakkuk was a younger contemporary of Isaiah; others place him later, as a younger contemporary of Jeremiah.

In his book, Habakkuk complains against the cruelties and inhumanities of the oppressors. Their continued victories and successes seem to him inconsistent with God's justice. God's response is that evil shall ultimately perish from the earth, and the upright shall live by their faithfulness.

Subject Matter and Book Synopsis

The language in the book is filled with metaphor and vivid imagery. The book itself begins on a note of challenge to God's justice and ends with confidence and faith that the righteous will continue to prevail and live by their faith.

The narrative of chapters 1 and 2 of the Book of Habakkuk consists of a series of five prophetic utterances. The first one (1:2-4) is a complaint against God for allowing injustice to prevail. The second utterance (1:5-11) is a Divine oracle prophesying that the instrument of judgment, namely, the Chaldeans, is close at hand. The third utterance (1:12-17) asks why God allows the wicked to prevail over the righteous, to which the fourth utterance (2:1-5) responds: eventually, the wicked shall fail, but the righteous shall live by their faith. The fifth utterance (2:7-20) takes the form of a series of parables that stress the punishment that the wicked will receive. Here God's glory is beautifully contrasted with the lifeless and dumb idols: "What profits the graven image, that the maker thereof has graven it, even the molten image, and the teacher of lies; that the maker of his work trusts therein to make dumb idols?" (2:18).

Chapter 3 comprises the prayer of the Prophet Habakkuk. A small part of the prayer is a petition, while the rest of it is a graphic vision in which God appears as a warrior armed with weapons of battle and a powerful army of followers. In the prayer, Habakkuk entreats the return of God's compassion and mercy. The prayer itself refers to God's actions at the time of the Exodus from Egypt. After re-counting the past, the prophet looks to the future and prays: "May I be relieved on the day of trouble, when the Chaldeans invade with their troops" (3:16). Habakkuk concludes by describing the effect of drought (3:17) while expressing his hope and faith: "Yea, I will rejoice in God and exult in the God of my salvation" (3:18).

Unlike Jeremiah and Ezekiel, who spent a great deal of time reiterating the sins of the people, Habbakuk directs his attack upon the sins of the enemy, which are more deplorable than even the backsliding of the Israelites.

Habbakuk in Rabbinic Literature

1. In the *Seder Olam*, it is told that Joel, Nachum, and Habbakuk all prophesied in the days of Manasseh (698–642 B.C.E.), and because of the wickedness of that king, his name was omitted from their books.

2. Habakkuk is included among the eight who prophesied after the destruction of the Temple, the others being Amos, Zephaniah, Haggai, Zechariah, Malachi, Micah, and Ezekiel (*Pesikta DeRav Kahana*).

3. According to legend, Habakkuk was the son of the Shunammite woman (Zohar 1:7).

4. In the apocryphal story of Bel and the Dragon, Habakkuk is introduced as a contemporary of Daniel.

5. According to Rabbi Simlai, a second-century scholar, Habakkuk based all of the 613 commandments received by Moses on the single principle that "the righteous shall live by his faith" (Habbakuk 2:4) (Talmud, *Makkot* 23b–24a).

Main Teachings and Concepts

1. Righteous people live by their faith: According to Habakkuk, righteous people, who remain loyal to the ethical and moral precepts, will endure, although they may have to at times suffer for their principles. The wicked, on the other hand, who may enjoy a temporary ascendancy through their violation of right, are in the end doomed to be destroyed.

2. Despite hardship, one must continue to stay confident: At the end of his book, Habakkuk, though alarmed at God's coming to deal out judgment, is full of confidence in Israel's ultimate salvation. In spite of severe hardships, the prophet, speaking for the people, will rejoice in God, confident that these hard times are only temporary: "Yet I will rejoice in God, I will exult in the God of my salvation. God, the Lord is my strength, and He makes my feet like hinds' feet and He makes me to walk upon the high places" (Habakkuk 3:18–19).

3. Idols are nonentities: Habbakuk contrasts God's glory with the uselessness of an idol: "Woe to the person that says to wood: 'Awake,' to the dumb

stone: 'Arise!' Can this teach? Behold, it is overlaid with gold and silver, and there is no breath at all in the midst of it" (Habakkuk 2:19).

Notable Quotations

1. How long, O God, shall I cry, and You will not hear? I cry out to You of violence, and You will not save (Habakkuk 1:2).

2. Are You not from everlasting, O Lord my God, my Holy One? We shall not die, O God. You have ordained them for judgment, and You, O Rock, have established them for correction (Habakkuk 1:12).

3. Behold, his soul is puffed up, it is not upright in him; but the righteous shall live by his faith (Habakkuk 2:4).

4. What profits the graven image, that the maker has graven it. Even the molten image, and the teacher of lies; that the maker of his work trusts therein, to make dumb idols? (Habakkuk 2:18).

5. God, the Lord is my strength, and He makes my feet like hinds' feet, and He makes me to walk upon my high places (Habakkuk 3:19).

Zephaniah

Composition and Authorship

Zephaniah, meaning "God has hidden," is the ninth book of the Books of the Minor Prophets. Zephaniah is an older contemporary of Jeremiah and lived in Jerusalem during the reign of King Josiah. There are no recorded details about him except for his lineage. Zephaniah was the great-great-grandson of King Hezekiah.

Zephaniah, who was one of the first persons to break the long silence of more than fifty years that followed the death of the Prophet Isaiah, condemned the pro-Assyrian court ministers who served as regents during Josiah's minority. His prophecy, therefore, comes directly before that of Jeremiah, who is said to have been influenced by it in both language and ideas. Unlike Amos and Micah, who championed the causes of the poor, Zechariah's main concern was with the downfall of all of the wicked nations, Judah included, and the salvation of the remnant of Israel that would carry on the chain of Jewish survival.

The brief three-chapter book stresses the demand for purity of heart and conduct. It also contains the idea that suffering has a disciplinary value. Zephaniah's prophecy was occasioned by the Scythian invasion of western Asia, which marked the beginning of the end to the Assyrian empire. In his book, Zephaniah pictures the approaching calamity in graphic terms and predicts the future glory of Jerusalem: "I will utterly consume all things from off the face of the earth, says God. I will consume human and beast, I will consume the fowls of the heaven, and the fish of the sea, and the stumbling blocks with the wicked. And I will cut off man from the face of the earth, says God" (Zephaniah 1:2–3).

Subject Matter and Book Synopsis

CHAPTER 1: BEGINS WITH A GATHERING OF ALL THE INHABITANTS OF THE WORLD AND THE PEOPLE OF JUDAH AND JERUSALEM FOR JUDGMENT AND TOTAL DESTRUCTION; IT IS BASICALLY A REVERSAL OF THE CREATION STORY IN THE FIRST CHAPTER OF THE BOOK OF GENESIS

1:2–18   The approach of God's judgment on the world

CHAPTER 2:
DOOM OF THE NATIONS OF THE PHILISTINES, MOAB, AMMON, AND ASSYRIA

2:1–4   Judah is urged to repent
2:5–7   Doom of the Philistines
2:8–11   Doom of Moab and Ammon
2:13–15   Doom of Assyria

CHAPTER 3: ORACLE OF WOE AGAINST JERUSALEM AND ITS LEADERS

3:1–7   Jerusalem is arraigned
3:8–13   Encouragement to the faithful
3:14–20   Judah and Jerusalem are bidden to sing

Major Concepts and Teachings

1. Importance of being nationalistic: Like many of the other prophets, Zephaniah was an ardent nationalist. He lashed out against those who were bent on assimilation, sacrificing their heritage for worthless things. He also condemned luxury and the pursuit of wealth for its own sake, declaring that salvation will spring forth from the humble and impoverished.

2. Importance of repentance: In chapter 2, Judah is urged to repent and exhorted not to despair of God's protection, even in the face of the coming

disaster: "Seek the Lord, all you humble of the earth that have executed God's ordinance; seek righteousness and seek humility: it may be that you will be hid in the day of God's anger" (Zephaniah 2:3).

3. Israel will in the future be saved: One of the most beautiful passages in all of the Book of Zephaniah occurs at the end, in which Israel is depicted as chastened and humbled, surviving the catastrophe in order to be able to worship the God of their ancestors in peaceful serenity. The goal of salvation has a cosmic sense in which all people, purified and humbled, will call upon the name of God and worship at His holy mountain.

Notable Quotations

1. I will utterly consume all things from off the face of the earth, says God (Zephaniah 1:1).

2. Seek God, all you humble of the earth, that have executed His ordinance; seek righteousness and humility: it may be that you shall be hid in the day of the Lord's anger (Zephaniah 2:3).

3. God Who is righteousness in the midst of her, He will not do unrighteousness; every morning does God bring His right to light. It does not fail, but the unrighteous knows no shame (Zephaniah 3:5).

4. Sing, O daughter of Zion, shout O Israel; be glad and rejoice with all of your heart, O daughter of Jerusalem (3:14).

Haggai

Composition and Authorship

The Book of Haggai (meaning "born on a festival") is the tenth book of the Minor Prophets, consisting of four prophecies delivered within the space of four months in 520 B.C.E. A contemporary of Zechariah and Malachi, Haggai is one of the last three literary prophets. His prophetic activity occurred eighteen years after Cyrus of Persia had permitted the exiles to return to Judea. The work of rebuilding the Temple had been at a standstill for seventeen years, because of the hostile Samaritans who had interfered with the work of the restoration.

Of the personal life of Haggai, next to nothing is known. There is no genealogy attached to his name. It does appear, however, that the prophet was previously well-known to the people. The author of Ezra-Nehemiah notes the important role he played in the rebuilding of the Temple in Jerusalem (Ezra 5:1, 6:14).

Haggai's prophecies deal mainly with the construction of the Temple and with the major events that the nation will experience in the future as a result of the presence of a Temple.

Subject Matter and Synopsis

Haggai sent four messages urging the exiles to rebuild the Temple in Jerusalem. He roused the energies and aspirations of the people who started a new life in Judea: "You who saw the Temple in its former splendor, what do you think of it now? You think nothing of it? Yet, take courage . . . work, for I am with you. Once again the treasures of all nations shall come in, and I will fill this house with splendor. The silver is mine, the gold is mine . . . upon this place I will bestow prosperity" (Haggai 2:3–8).

Haggai's unadorned prose reflects the wretched situation of Jerusalem prior to the arrival of Nehemiah, governor of Jerusalem. His strong self-reliance, combined with a serene trust in God, contributed to his success in fortifying Jerusalem both physically and spiritually against the surrounding enemies of his people.

Here is a brief synopsis of the book, chapter by chapter:

1:1–11   An appeal to rebuild the Temple
1:12–15   The response of the people
2:1–9   The greater glory of the Second Temple

2:10–19   Promise of an immediate change for
                 the better

Haggai in Rabbinic Tradition

According to talmudic tradition, Haggai, Zechariah, and Malachi were the founders of the Great
Synagogue and influenced Jonathan ben Uzziel in
his Aramaic translation of the Books of the Prophets. Talmudic tradition also declares that with the
death of Haggai, Zechariah, and Malachi, the Holy
Spirit departed from Israel. Finally, the rabbis in
the talmudic tractate of *Bava Batra* 15a attributed
the editing of the Book of Haggai to the Men of the
Great Assembly.

Major Concepts and Teachings

1. The Temple must be rebuilt in order to usher in
the dawn of the Kingdom of God: Haggai speaks
encouragingly to the leaders, Zerubbabel and
Joshua, and earnestly calls upon the people to
devote themselves to the holy task of building the
new Temple. He furthermore asserts that the glory
of this Temple will be greater than that of the
former Temple (Haggai 2:9).

2. God's covenant with the Israelites is eternal: In
chapter 2:5, God is quoted as saying that the cov-

enant He made with the Israelites is still binding and in force.

3. The transmitting power of impurity is greater than that of holiness: In chapter 2:13, Haggai asks this question of the priests: "If one that is unclean by a dead body touch any of these, shall it be unclean?" The priests answered, "yes." Haggai then applies the ruling to the Israelites. He asserts that just as the transmitting power of impurity is greater than that of holiness, so it is with the Israelites. The wicked (i.e., those indifferent to the neglect of the Temple) can readily taint while the righteous (i.e., those zealous for the restoration of the Temple) cannot so eagerly influence the wicked.

Notable Quotations

1. You have sown much, and brought in little, you eat but you have enough. You drink, but are not filled with drink. You clothe, but there is none warm. And he that earns wages earns them for a bag with holes (Haggai 1:6).

2. The word that I covenanted with you when you came out of Egypt have I established, and My spirit abides among you. Do not be afraid (Haggai 2:5).

3. The glory of this latter house will be greater than that of the former, says the Lord of Hosts; and

in this place will I give peace, says the Lord of Hosts (Haggai 2:9).

4. . . . . "If one that is unclean by a dead body touch any of these, shall it be unclean?" And the priests answered and said: "It shall be unclean" (Haggai 2:13).

Zechariah

Composition and Authorship

The Book of Zechariah is the eleventh of the Twelve Minor Prophets, consisting of fourteen chapters. The most characteristic feature of the book is his visions, by which Zechariah expresses the truths he received from God. The visions are often accompanied by direct or indirect explanations made by the angel who speaks to him and who serves as an intermediary between the prophet and God. Zechariah's prophecies, like those of Ezekiel, are apocalyptic. The purpose of his night visions is to teach of the future purification of Jerusalem.

The first eight chapters, generally referred to as part one, contain a series of eight visions, by means of which the prophet expresses his assurance that God will restore Israel's former glory. The last six chapters, often spoken of as part two, include prophecies concerning the coming of the Messiah, deliverance, final victory, and God's reign of peace.

Some Bible scholars are of the opinion that the last six chapters belong to a much earlier anonymous author, a "Second Zechariah"; others, however, maintain that the so-called Second Zechariah lived at a much later period than the original Zechariah, who, like his older contemporary Haggai, urged the immediate rebuilding of the Jerusalem Temple during the years 520–518 before the Common Era. Unlike Haggai, Zechariah attributes the destruction of the Temple and the exile to sin and connects redemption with repentance.

The introduction to the book attributes the work to Zechariah, son of Berechiah, son of Iddo the prophet (Zechariah 1:1 and 1:7). The prophet's name is also mentioned in the Book of Ezra (5:1 and 6:14). Zechariah began to prophesy in the month of *Kislev*, during the second year of Darius's reign. In addition to urging the Israelites to return to Zion in order to complete the building of the Temple, he also prophesied the ingathering of the exiles and Israel's liberation from foreign bondage.

Subject Matter and Synopsis

The historical setting for the Book of Zechariah is similar to that of the Book of Haggai. The Jewish people, who had returned from the Babylonian exile, immediately set about the task of restoring the Temple. No sooner had the work begun than it was stopped on account of hostile neighbors. In the second year of the reign of Darius, the work resumed. It was left to Zechariah to bring the task to completion.

As was previously mentioned, the most characteristic features of Zechariah's prophecies are his visions. With Zechariah, angels as God's messengers are a constant feature, and the angel plays an important role in explaining the many visions to the prophet.

The visions in the book portray the working of God in the world. They depict the restoration of the exiles into a community, they announce the overthrow of the heathen nations, and they depict the new Jerusalem as a city of peace. They express the need for Divine forgiveness and foretell the removal of iniquity from God's people.

Chapters 1–6 contain eight visions. In the first of them (1:8–17), one night Zechariah sees a man astride a red horse stranded among myrtle trees. Behind him are red, sorrel, and white horses. The angel explains that the horses symbolize messengers sent throughout the world by God to see what is transpiring. They return with the information that all is tranquil. The angel, seemingly disappointed, then prays for the rebuilding of Jerusalem and the cities of Judah that have aroused God's anger.

In one of the most famous visions (chapter 4:1–7), of a seven-branched candlestick, Zechariah's thoughts turn to Zerubbabel and the need to encourage him in his work:

And the angel that spoke with me returned, and awakened me, as a man that is wakened out of his sleep. And he said to me: "What do you see?" And I said: "I have seen, and behold a candlestick all of gold, with a bowl on the top of it, and its seven lamps thereon . . . and two olive trees by it, one upon the right side of the bow, and the other on the left." And I answered and spoke to the angel that spoke with me saying: "What are these, my lord?" Then the angel that spoke with me answered and said to me: "You do not know what these are?" Then he answered and spoke to me, saying: "This is the word of the Lord unto Zerubbabel, saying: Not by might, nor by power, but by My spirit, says the Lord of Hosts."

This passage is traditionally recited as the prophetic portion on the Sabbath of Hannukah. The lesson here is that God alone is the source of all light, as well as power, to rulers and people alike. The Bible commentator Kimchi posits that the two olive trees represent Joshua and Zerubbabel, who were appointed respectively to the spiritual and civil leadership, and by whom the work in hand would be accomplished. Finally, the famous line "not by might nor by power, but by My Spirit, says the Lord of Hosts" implies that success depends not upon brute strength and human power but upon the Divine Spirit.

The entire second section of the Book of Zechariah lacks any mention of the prophet's name and period. There are no visions, and no angels appear in these chapters. No allusion is made to the rebuilding of the Temple. Instead, new topics are introduced, including the threatened punishment of Tyre and the Philistines, the denouncement of Judah's governors, the belittling of diviners, and

the capture of Jerusalem and her subsequent deliverance.

Here is a synopsis of the Book of Zechariah:

1:1–6	Call to repentance
1:7–6:15	Eight visions of Zechariah and their interpretations
1:7–17	First Vision: The Heavenly Horses
2:1–4	Second Vision: Four Horns and Four Craftsmen
2:5–9	Third Vision: The Man with the Measuring Line
2:10–17	An Interlude: Appeal to the exiles to return
3:1–10	Fourth Vision: Charge against Joshua and His Vindication by God
4:1–4	Fifth Vision: Golden Lamp and a Promise to Zerubbabel
5:1–4	Sixth Vision: The Flying Scroll
5:5–11	Seventh Vision: The Woman in the Measure
6:1–8	Eighth Vision: Four Chariots
6:9–15	Coronation scene
7:1–7	Deportation to enquire about the fasts
7:8–14	Summary of the teachings of the former prophets
8:1–23	Ten Divine Messages: (1) God's earnestness for the restoration of Zion; (2) God's Presence in Zion; (3) Jerusalem, the scene of joyous youth; (4) "Is anything too wondrous for God?"; (5) The Great Ingathering; (6) The anxious times are past with the restoration of the Temple; (7) Demand of

	social righteousness; (8) Solemn fasts will become cheerful ones; (9) Attractive power of true religion of God; (10) Worldwide renown of the Jew.
9:1–8	Incorporation of neighboring states into new kingdom of Israel
9:9–10	The king of peace
9:11–12	Return of the exiles
9:13–17	Victory in the future of Jews over the Greeks
10:1–2	Prosperity comes from God
10:3–12	Restoration of Israel and Judah
11:1–3	Lament over the doom of the nations
11:4–14	Rejection of the divinely appointed shepherd
11:15–17	Worthless shepherd is appointed as a punishment
12:1–9	Deliverance of Jerusalem
12:10–14	Mourning over a martyr
13:1–6	Purgation of Judah
13:7–9	Fate of the shepherd and his flock
14:1–11	Deliverance of Jerusalem
14:12–15	The great plague
14:16–21	In the future all will worship One God

Zechariah in Rabbinic Writings

Zechariah was one of the three prophets to accompany the exiles who returned from Babylon to Jerusalem. His contribution to the rebuilding of the Temple consisted of his testimony regarding the siting of the altar (Talmud, *Zevachim* 62a). He prophesied together with Haggai and Malachi in the second year of the reign of Darius (Talmud, *Megillah* 15a). He could also interpret difficult biblical texts (Talmud, *Eruvin* 21a–b). Like Haggai and Malachi, he received his learning directly from the early prophets (*Avot De Rabbi Natan* 1:1). It was after the death of Zechariah, Haggai, and Malachi that the Holy Spirit departed from Israel (Talmud, *Yoma* 9b). Finally, according Maimonides, Zechariah received the tradition from Baruch, son of Neriah, and his court.

Major Concepts and Teachings

1. Temple service and sacrifices were only a means to an end: For Zechariah, the Temple service and its accompanying ritual was only a means to an end. That end was the establishment of God's Kingdom on earth. Thus, Zechariah urged the people to practice justice and kindness and preached that fasting and other ritual cannot take the place of ethical character.

2. Belief in God would in the future spread throughout the nations and all idolatry would come to an end: One day in the future, according to the Book of Zechariah, monotheism will be universal, and the Eternal God alone will be everywhere acknowledged and worshiped. Zechariah declared that "in those days it shall come to pass, that ten men shall . . . take hold of the skirt of him that is a Jew, saying: We will go with you, for we have heard that

God is with you" (Zechariah 8:13). However, such happenings would have to be preceded by whole-hearted repentance on the part of the people. "These are the things that you shall do. Speak every person the truth with his neighbor, execute the judgment of truth and peace in your gates; and let none of you devise evil in your hearts against his neighbor, and love no false oath" (Zechariah 8:16,17). "And God shall be King over all the earth; in that day shall God be One and His name one" (Zechariah 14:9).

3. Spirit is more important than brute force: According to the Book of Zechariah, it is the spirit of the Divine Force rather than use of physical force that can help people accomplish important tasks in life. This is based on the famous verse in the book "not by might, nor by power, but by My Spirit, says the Lord of Hosts" (Zechariah 4:6). These words may be said to proclaim the lesson of all of Jewish history. It is also the prophetic teaching of the Maccabean festival of Hanukkah, in which the small band of Maccabees against great odds was able to defeat a much larger and stronger Syrian-Greek enemy.

4. Prosperity is from God alone: God is the Lord of Nature and is responsible for seasonal rains that provide for the bounteous growth of crops. Chapter 10:1 best sums up this teaching with these words: "Ask of God rain in the time of the latter rain; even of the Lord that makes lightnings, and God will give them showers of rain, to every one grass in the field."

Notable Quotations

1. Sing and rejoice, O daughter of Zion; for lo, I come, and I will dwell in the midst of you, says God (Zechariah 2:14).

2. Thus says the Lord of Hosts: If you will walk in My ways, and if you will keep My charge, and will also judge My house, and will also keep My courts, then I will give you free access among these that stand by (Zechariah 3:8).

3. . . . Not by might, nor by power, but by My spirit, says the Lord of Hosts (Zechariah 4:6).

4. Thus has the Lord of Hosts spoken, saying: Execute true judgment, and show mercy and compassion every person to his brother (Zechariah 7:9).

5. And the Lord shall be King over all the earth, and on that day the Lord shall be One, and His Name One (Zechariah 14:9).

Malachi

Composition and Authorship

The Book of Malachi ("my messenger," in Hebrew) is the last book of the Twelve Minor Prophets. Nowhere else in the Bible does the name "Malachi" occur, and thus it has been questioned whether it is the personal name of the prophet. The *Targum* identifies Malachi with Ezra, the Scribe.

This unidentified prophet, who was active about the middle of the fifth century before the Common Era, stresses personal religion and emphasizes mercy and faith. He analyzes the proper way of life and deals with questions that have to be faced repeatedly.

The Socratic method of developing an idea through question and answer is a prominent feature of Malachi's style: "A son should honor his father, and a servant should honor his master. Now, if I am a Father, where is my honor? If I am a Master, where is my reverence? . . . Have we not

197

all one Father? Has not one God created us? Why then, are we faithless to one another?" (Malachi 1:6, 2:10).

Subject Matter and Synopsis

From the conditions described in the book, one may reasonably conclude that the Prophet Malachi ministered in Jerusalem before the advent of Ezra and Nehemiah. We learn from the rebuke passed by Malachi that the Temple service had fallen into disgrace. The priests had grown careless of their religious duties and the people grew negligent in their payment of tithes. Morality was lax, divorce and intermarriage common. The task before Malachi was to arouse the Israelites from their apathy and rekindle in them the true spirit of religiosity. He passionately denounces the moral wrongdoings of the time, pronouncing doom on sorcerers, adulterers, and those who oppress the widow and orphan (Malachi 3:5).

The people addressed throughout the Book of Malachi are divided into two classes: the sincerely devout who are beginning to question Divine goodness in view of the prevailing evil; and the greedy men who are devout only in name.

Malachi also announces the impending Day of the Lord. It is to be a day of judgment for Israel, when God will pass His people through the fire of the refiner, removing the dross of evil from the previous metal. God will then bring to light the truly righteous, and the wicked will be consumed.

This Day of the Lord will come with warning: "Behold, I will send you Elijah the Prophet before the coming of the great and terrible Day of the Lord. And he shall turn the heart of the fathers to the children, and the heart of the children to their father; lest I come and smite the land with utter destruction" (Malachi 3:23–24).

It is Elijah who will prepare the way for the coming of the Lord and restore harmony in the homes of the people, turning their hearts to God.

Here is a synopsis of the Book of Malachi, chapter by chapter:

1:1–5	God's love for Israel is proved by the contrasted fortunes of Israel and Edom
1:6–2:9	Arraignment of the Priests
2:10–16	Protest against divorce and intermarriage
2:17–3:6	Approach of the Day of Judgment
3:7–12	Payment of tithes wins the favor of God
3:13–21	Doom of the wicked and triumph of the righteous
3:22–24	Elijah, the Prophet, will announce the coming of the Messiah

Malachi in Rabbinic Writings

The author of Malachi was considered one of the last prophets, along with Haggai and Zechariah. Upon their deaths, the spirit of prophecy departed from Israel (Talmud, *Yoma* 9b). Malachi was identified with Ezra by Rabbi Joshua ben Korcha and with Mordecai by Rabbi Nachman. The sages, however, declared that Malachi was his proper name (Talmud, *Megillah* 15a). Malachi was a member of the Great Synagogue, and traditions were later reported in his name (Talmud, *Rosh Hashanah* 19b).

Major Concepts and Teachings

1. The prosperity of the Israelite people is dependent upon the observance of Temple ritual, which must give rise to high ethical standards: Malachi condemns the moral wrongs of his time, especially speaking out with much passion against divorce and intermarriage as acts of treachery against God and the nation.

2. God is a God to all people: In his denunciation of the stinginess of his people in the matter of sacrifices to God, Malachi holds aloft as a contrast the respect shown to Him by the heathens in their offerings. Malachi recognizes that all sincere heathen worship is in reality offered to the One God of all the earth: "For from the rising of the sun even unto the going down of the same, My name is great among the nations; and in every place offerings are presented unto My name; even pure oblations, for My name is great among the nations, says God" (Malachi 1:11).

3. In the end of days, the wicked will be doomed to destruction and the righteous will triumph: Ac-

cording to the Book of Malachi, a day in the future will come that will bring ultimate salvation to the world. Elijah, the Prophet, is the one who will prepare the way for the coming of the Lord. When he comes, he will turn the hearts of the fathers to the children and the hearts of the children to their fathers. Thus, the family discord that had resulted from divorces and foreign marriages will be alleviated, and harmony in the homes will return.

Notable Quotations

1. A son honors his father, and a servant his master; if then I be a father, where is My honor; and if I be a master, where is My fear? says the Lord of Hosts . . . (Malachi 1:6).

2. Have we not all one father? Has not one God created us? Why do we deal treacherously every person against his brother, profaning the covenant of our ancestors? (Malachi 2:10).

3. Behold, I will send you Elijah the Prophet, before the coming of the great and terrible day of the Lord. And he shall turn the heart of the fathers to the children, and the heart of the children to their fathers; lest I come and smite the land with utter destruction (Malachi 3:23–24).

IV

The *Haftarah*— The Lesson from the Prophets

15

Overview

The *Haftarah* refers to the prophetical section recited after the reading of the Torah on Sabbaths,
festivals, and fast days. Selections are either from
the so-called "Earlier Prophets" (Joshua, Judges,
Samuel, and Kings) or from the "Later Prophets"
(Isaiah, Jeremiah, Ezekiel, and the Book of the
Twelve Prophets). Although we possess no historical data concerning the institution of these lessons, it is believed that this tradition began in
ancient Palestine in the second century B.C.E. when
the Syrians had forbidden the reading of the Torah. Selections from the Prophets, usually bearing
a theme linked to an incident mentioned in the
assigned Torah reading, were therefore substituted. Even when the *Haftarah* does not contain an
explicit reference to the events of the Torah reading, it generally reinforces the teaching of the
weekly reading upon the mind of the worshiper by
a prophetic message of consolation and hope.

In time, the reading of the *Haftarah* became a
regular part of Sabbath and festival services. On

the three Sabbaths preceding the fast of the Ninth of *Av*, the day commemorating the destruction of the Temple, prophecies of rebuke are recited, whereas on the seven Sabbaths after the Ninth of *Av*, the *Haftarah* consists of prophetic utterances of comfort and consolation.

Rabbi David Abudarham, of fourteenth-century Spain, in his commentary on liturgy, traces the custom of reading from the Prophets after the Torah reading back to the period of persecution preceding the Maccabean revolt. According to his theory, the *Haftarah* was introduced as a substitute for the Torah reading, which had been prohibited under the severe decrees of Antiochus Epiphanes.

Several rabbinic authorities suggest that the readings from the Prophets may have been instituted to emphasize the great value of these books to the Torah of Moses. This was done in order to oppose the Samaritans, who refused to recognize the sanctity of the Prophets. This sect, which originated in the early years of the Second Temple in the district of Samaria, Palestine, strictly observed the precepts of the Five Books of Moses but rejected not only rabbinic interpretation and tradition but also the prophetical writings.

Special signs of cantillation or accents (known in Hebrew as *ta'amei hamikrah*) have been placed both above and under the Hebrew words of the *Haftarah* text. Their purpose is to serve both as musical notes and as marks of punctuation, thus indicating the logical relationships of words to each other. During the medieval period, it was generally believed that the signs of cantillation had been originated by Ezra, the Scribe, and the members of the Great Assembly, who flourished several centuries before the Common Era. The members of the Great Assembly were a body of spiritual leaders, described as the successors of the prophets in keeping alive the knowledge of the Torah. Aaron ben Asher, the tenth-century masoretic scholar of Tiberias, who devoted many years to preparing an accurate Bible manuscript with all the traditional marks of vocalization and cantillation, speaks of the accents as the contribution of the prophets themselves, to whom the interpretation of every word was revealed.

16

Summary of Bible Portions

Following is a summary of each of the Bible portions throughout the year, along with their corresponding readings in both the Five Books of Moses and the prophetic texts.

Name	Torah Text		Prophetic Reading
Bereishit	Genesis	1:1–6:8	Isaiah 42:5–43:11 (42:5–21)
Noach		6:9–11:32	Isaiah 54:1–55:5 (54:1–10)
Lech Lecha		12:1–17:27	Isaiah 40:27–41:16
Vayera		18:1–22:24	2 Kings 4:1–37 (4:1–23)
Chayei Sarah		23:1–25:18	1 Kings 1:1–31
Toledot		25:19–28:9	Malachi 1:1–2:7
Vayetzei		28:10–32:3	Hosea 12:12–14:10 (11:7–12:12)
Vayishlach		32:4–36:43	Hosea 11:17–12:12 (Obadiah 1:1–21)
Vayeshev		37:1–40:23	Amos 2:6–3:8
Miketz		41:1–44:17	1 Kings 3:15–4:1
Vayigash		44:18–47:27	Ezekiel 37:15–25

Name		Torah Text	Prophetic Reading
Vayechi		47:28–50:26	1 Kings 2:1–12
Shemot	Exodus	1:1–6:1	Isaiah 27:6–28:13; 29:22–23
			(Jeremiah 1:1–2:3)
Vaeyra		6:2–9:35	Ezekiel 28:25–29:21
Bo		10:1–13:16	Jeremiah 46:13–28
Beshallach		13:17–17:16	Judges 4:4–5:31 (5:1–31)
Yitro		18:1–20:23	Isaiah 6:1–7:6; 9:5–6
			(6:1–13)
Mishpatim		21:1–24:18	Jeremiah 34:8–22; 33:25–26
Terumah		25:1–27:19	1 Kings 5:26–6:13
Tetzaveh		27:20–30:10	Ezekiel 43:10–27
Ki Tisa		30:11–34:35	1 Kings 18:1–39
			(18:20–39)
Vayakhel		35:1–38:20	1 Kings 7:40–50 (7:13–26)
Pekudei		38:21–40:38	1 Kings 7:51–8:21
			(7:40–50)
Vayikra	Leviticus	1:1–5:26	Isaiah 43:21–44:23
Tzav		6:1–8:36	Jeremiah 7:21–8:3; 9:22–23
Shemini		9:1–11:47	2 Samuel 6:1–7:17
			(6:1–19)
Tazria		12:1–13:59	2 Kings 4:42–5:19
Metzora		14:1–15:33	2 Kings 7:3–20
Acharei Mot		16:1–18:30	Ezekiel 22:1–19 (22:1–16)
Kedoshim		19:1–20:27	Amos 9:7–15
			(Ezekiel 20:2–20)
Emor		21:1–24:23	Ezekiel 44:15–31
Behar		25:1–26:2	Jeremiah 32:6–27
Bechukotai		26:3–27:34	Jeremiah 16:19–17:14
Bemidbar	Numbers	1:1–4:20	Hosea 2:1–22
Naso		4:21–7:89	Judges 13:2–25
Behaalotecha		8:1–12:16	Zechariah 2:14–4:7
Shelach		13:1–15:41	Joshua 2:1–24

Name	Torah Text	Prophetic Reading
Korach	16:1–18:32	1 Samuel 11:14–12:22
Chukat	19:1–22:1	Judges 11:1–33
Balak	22:2–25:9	Micah 5:6–6:8
Pinchas	25:10–30:1	1 Kings 18:46–19:21
Mattot	30:2–32:42	Jeremiah 1:1–2:3
Masey	33:1–36:13	Jeremiah 2:4–28; 3:4 (2:4–28; 4:1–2)
Devarim	Deuteronomy 1:1–3:22	Isaiah 1:1–27
Va-etchanan	3:23–7:11	Isaiah 40:1–26
Ekev	7:12–11:25	Isaiah 49:14–51:3
Re'eh	11:26–16:17	Isaiah 54:11–55:5
Shofetim	16:18–21:9	Isaiah 51:12–52:12
Ki Tetze	21:10–25:19	Isaiah 54:1–10
Ki Tavo	26:1–29:8	Isaiah 60:1–22
Nitzavim	29:9–30:20	Isaiah 61:10–63:9
Vayelech	31:1–30	Isaiah 55:6–56:8
Haazinu	32:1–52	2 Samuel 22:1–51
Vezot Ha-berachah	33:1–34:12	Joshua 1:1–18 (1:1–9)

Note: Parentheses indicate Sephardic ritual

Special Readings

Rosh Hashanah	1st Day	Genesis 21:1–34; Numbers 29:1–6	1 Samuel 1:1–2:10
	2nd Day	Genesis 22:1–24; Numbers 29:1–6	Jeremiah 31:2–20
Shabbat Shuvah		Weekly portion	Hosea 14:2–10; Micah 7:18–20 or Hosea 14:2–10; (Hosea 14:2–10; Micah 7:18–20)
Yom Kippur	Morning	Leviticus 16:1–34; Numbers 29:7–11	Isaiah 57:14–58:14

Special Readings

Sukkot	1st Day	Leviticus 22:26–23:44;	Zechariah 14:1–21
		Numbers 29:12–16	
	2nd Day	Leviticus 22:26–23:44;	1 Kings 8:2–21
		Numbers 29:12–16	
Shabbat Chol Hamoed Sukkot		Exodus 33:12–34:26;	Ezekiel 38:18–39:16
		Daily portion from Numbers 29	
	8th Day	Deuteronomy 14:22–16:17;	1 Kings 8:56–66
		Numbers 29:35–30:1	
Simchat Torah		Deuteronomy 33:1–34:12;	Joshua 1:1–18
		Genesis 1:1–2:3	(1:1–9)
		Numbers 29:35–30:1	
1st *Shabbat* Chanukah		Weekly and Chanukah portions	Zechariah 2:14–4:7
2nd *Shabbat* Chanukah		Weekly and Chanukah portions	1 Kings 7:40–50
Shabbat Shekalim		Weekly portion; Exodus 30:11–16	2 Kings 12:1–17 (11:17–12:17)
Shabbat Zachor		Weekly portion; Deuteronomy 25:17–19	1 Samuel 15:2–34 (15:1–34)
Shabbat Parah		Weekly portion; Numbers 19:1–22	Ezekiel 36:16–38 (36:16–36)
Shabbat Hachodesh		Weekly portion; Exodus 12:1–20	Ezekiel 45:16–46:18 (45:18–46:15)
Shabbat Hagadol		Weekly portion	Malachi 3:4–24
Pesach	1st Day	Exodus 12:21–51; Numbers 28:16–25	Joshua 3:5–7; 5:2–6:1; 6:27 (5:2–6:1)

Special Readings

	2nd Day	Leviticus 22:26–23:44; Numbers 28:16–25	2 Kings 23:1–9; 21–25
Shabbat Pesach		Exodus 33:12–34:26; Numbers 28:19–25	Ezekiel 36:37–37:14 (37:1–14)
	7th Day	Exodus 13:17–15:26; Numbers 28:19–25	2 Samuel 22:1–51
	8th Day	Deuteronomy 15:19–16:17; (on *Shabbat* 14:22–16:17) Numbers 28:19–25	Isaiah 10:32–12:6
Shavuot	1st Day	Exodus 19:11–23 Numbers 28:26–31	Ezekiel 1:1–28; 3:12
	2nd Day	Deuteronomy 15:19–16:17 (on *Shabbat* 14:22–6:17) Numbers 28:26–31	Habakkuk 3:1–19 (2:20–3:19)
Tisha B'Av	Morning	Deuteronomy 4:25–40	Jeremiah 8:13–9:23
	Afternoon	Exodus 32:11–14 34:1–10	Isaiah 55:6–56:8
Shabbat Rosh Chodesh		Weekly portion	Isaiah 66:1–24
Shabbat immediately preceding Rosh Chodesh		Weekly portion	1 Samuel 20:18–42

V

Prophecy and Jewish Philosophers

17

Overview

Jewish philosophers over the centuries have had much to say relative to the nature of prophecy and the Jewish prophet. Following is a brief synopsis of various Jewish philosophers and their thoughts related to prophets and prophecy.

18

Ancient Philosophy: Philo

Philo was an early first-century philosopher whose Greek writings primarily focused on the Torah. He conceived of the prophet to be a priest, seer, and lawgiver all wrapped up in one. According to Philo, prophetic understanding is the highest form, transcending reason. When the Divine spirit rests on a person, that person becomes "possessed" by it in a kind of frenzy. All prophecy is made available to humans through God's grace but prophecy through the Divine spirit, in contrast to communication through angels, demands a great deal of preparation. A person, in order to ready himself for prophecy, must be purified, wise, just, and liberated totally from all bodily concerns.

Although prophecy for Philo includes the power of predicting the future, still, the prophet's main function is to be the interpreter of God's will.

19

Medieval Philosophy

Maimonides

All medieval philosophers were concerned with prophecy and the manner and definition of a prophet, since the religious community defines itself by the revealed Divine law.

Maimonides defines prophecy as an overflow coming from God, through the Active Intellect, toward a person's rational faculty and then toward that person's imaginative faculty. For Maimonides, scientific understanding and imagination work together in prophecy, which explains why some prophetic writings are graphic while others are more abstract.

Since prophecy is an intellectual act, it can only come to a person with superior intellectual gifts and the discipline needed to perfect them. In addition, God must want a certain person to be a prophet, and He is therefore capable of preventing a person with superior intellectual gifts from becoming one. The general thrust of Maimonides is to restrict the range of people who are, or who could become, prophets.

Maimonides follows Jewish tradition (Deuteronomy 34:10) in arguing that Moses's prophecy is unique. He asserts that Moses, unlike most other prophets, was able to confront God directly. Thus, Moses is the only prophet who spoke to God "face to face" (Exodus 33:11). Whereas many prophets confronted God in dreams, Maimonides asserts that Moses was able to confront God in broad daylight.

With respect to non-Jewish prophets, Maimonides appears to think that if a Gentile perfected his or her soul to the required degree, prophetic illumination would be possible.

Saadia Gaon

This tenth-century philosopher sees a necessity for prophecy with respect to both rational and revealed commandments. Rational commandments are understood to be those required by reason whereas revealed ones are those given through revelation. The latter, Saadia says, must be accepted for no other reason than that they were proclaimed by God. In the case of revealed commandments, Saadia asserts that the prophet is God's instrument for apprising the community of God's will. In the case of rational commandments, the prophet's revelation augments, corrects, and reinforces human reason. For Saadia, verification of a prophet is confirmed by the miracles he works, but such confirmation can apply only to teaching that accords with reason. Miracles, by themselves, do not confirm a prophet whose message is preposterous or rationally impossible.

Judah HaLevi

Judah HaLevi, in his work *The Kuzari*, stresses the distinctiveness of the children of Israel and the Land of Israel. All the chosen people in their chosen land sought to attain the level of prophecy, and many or most of them did in fact attain it.

For HaLevi, prophecy appears to be a gift. Preparation for prophecy is related to the performance of devout acts and a concern for purity. In this way men approach as near to God as is humanly possible, in the highest case coming to know "the meaning of *Adonai*." This knowledge of God is grasped through prophetic intuition, and its possessor is raised to the rank of angels.

Joseph Albo

The main features of Maimonides' views of prophecy are reaffirmed by this fifteenth-century philosopher. The absence of prophecy among the philosophers suggests to Albo that prophecy is not merely a natural consequence of investigative knowledge. Though the Divine overflow goes to the individu-

al's rational faculty, his preparedness is less critical than the Divine will to so favor a man. Albo
further asserts that neither divination of the future
nor the working of miracles most distinguishes
prophets. Finally, as did Maimonides, he posits
that Moses is the greatest of all prophets, having
reached the highest stage of prophecy—the ability
to be informed of the Divine rules by which one
may lead a nation to human perfection.

20

Modern Jewish Philosophers

Depending on their attitude toward revelation, modern Jewish philosophers treat prophecy either as a subjective experience or as a supernatural phenomenon. For those who treat it as a subjective experience, they either dismiss it as a form of psychological delusion or view it as a mystical experience deriving from intellectual or imaginative faculties. Of those treating prophecy as a supernatural phenomenon, some regard it as the authentic disclosure of a message received word by word from God, while others regard it as the record of a human response to a Divine revelation of content.

As a rationalist, the philosopher Moses Mendelssohn maintained that reason could supply a person with all the theoretical insights needed for salvation. Therefore, he restricted the function of prophecy to the practical sphere, to the Divine communication of instruction for human action.

Hermann Cohen regarded the prophets as pioneering thinkers who removed the mythical ele-

ments from religion and developed Judaism into a
universal ethical monotheism (i.e., belief in God
and adherence to moral law).

Naturalist thinkers, such as Mordecai Kaplan,
ruled out all supernatural elements in prophecy,
while Jewish existentialist thinkers, such as Martin Buber, characterize prophecy as a dialogue
relationship between man and God, rather than as
the disclosure of any message. For Buber, the
prophet's message reflects the prophet's personal
subjective response to his encounter with God.
Likewise in the view of Franz Rosenzweig, although revelation is a supernatural event occur-
ring at specific times to particular individuals, the
words of the prophet are purely the human interpretation of a revelatory experience in which God
reveals His love to human beings.

Of the most recent Orthodox thinkers, Joseph
Soloveitcik maintains that the prophetic encounter, a dialogue initiated by God, makes possible
what he terms the establishment of a "covenantal
community" between God and man.

Of all modern philosophers, Abraham Joshua
Heschel, one of the most influential modern philosophers of religion, spent a great deal of time on
the subject of prophecy, having written his doc-
toral dissertation on the subject. His unique contribution in this area related to his development of
the doctrine of what he called "Divine pathos" and
"Prophetic sympathy"—two individuating characteristics of Hebrew monotheism, as he understood
it. "Divine pathos" is the term Heschel uses to
characterize the openness of the Divine to human
action. The Bible shows us a God Who is a moral

personality Who is truly concerned with humankind, especially the people of Israel. The Bible
repeatedly presents an image of God and man and
God and Israel in terms of the covenant. When
Israel acts properly, God is happy, whereas when it
transgresses, God is angry and saddened. Heschel
argues that God is affected by human behavior,
feeling sympathy and pathos for people. This, posits Heschel, basically defines the prophetic con-
sciousness of God.

The human response to the Divine pathos is what
Heschel terms "prophetic sympathy." This refers
to the prophet's recognition of his relation to, and
influence upon, the Divine and the human situation
created thereby. In this situation, people, "sympa-
thetically" disposed toward God, willingly desire
to actively work to realize God's Will in order to
create a state of joyful Divine pathos. Aware of
God's sensitivity to human action, the mission of
the prophet is to call his people to do what is right
by God. Thus, both man and God are always in the
Jewish prophet's thoughts, at one and the same
time.

VI

Prophets in Jewish Liturgy

21

Sabbath and Festival Prayers

The prayerbook is replete with selected verses and sayings from the Books of the Prophets, as well as a prayer that includes a statement by one of the so-called seven heathen prophets. The following is a cross-section of those prophetic verses and sayings that appear in the daily, Sabbath, and Festival prayerbooks.

Ma Tovu

The first verse of the prayer *Ma Tovu*, which is used as the introductory prayer that opens the service, was originally recited by Balaam, a heathen prophet. Balaam was hired by Balak, King of Moab, to curse the Israelites. Instead, when he saw their beautifully arranged tents on a hilltop, he was compelled to bless the children of Israel with the words of *Ma Tovu*: "How beautiful are your tents, O Jacob, your dwelling places, O Israel"

(Numbers 24:5). Because the word "tents" was rabbinically understood to be referring to synagogues and "dwelling places" to schools, it became the custom to recite the words of *Ma Tovu* upon entering the synagogue.

Prayer for Donning Phylacteries

As a Jew wraps the straps of the phylacteries three times around the middle finger, he or she recites the following verse, taken from the Minor Prophet Hosea 2:21–22: "Thus says God: I will betroth you to Me forever. I will betroth you with righteousness, with justice, with love and with compassion. I will betroth you to Me with faithfulness, and you shall love the Lord."

When one dons *tefillin*, one is symbolically binding oneself to God. These verses were most likely chosen for this ritual act because they have the power to carry the Jew back to the revelation on Mount Sinai when God effected a "spiritual marriage" with Israel, with the Torah symbolizing the dowry. The threefold repetition of "I will betroth you" denotes affection and permanence.

Ata Hu Adonai Eloheynu

In the prayer *Ata Hu Adonai Elohenu*—You are the Lord, our God—which appears in the early part of the preliminary morning service, a verse appears that is directly taken from the Book of the Minor Prophet Zephaniah. It is the concluding verse of the book, chapter 3, verse 20: "At that time will I bring you in, and at that time I will gather you; for I will make you a name and a praise among all the peoples of the earth, when I bring back your captivity before your eyes, says the Lord."

Zephaniah was the prophet of world judgment and also the prophet of universal salvation. The implication of this most striking utterance is that the peoples of the earth were now dimly groping after the true God and only stammering His praise; but the time would come when they would adorn God with a full knowledge of Him, and, with one consent, form a universal chorus to chant God's praise. In that day Israel and Israel's Divine redemption would be both "a name and a praise among all the peoples of the earth."

Song of the Sea

The Song of the Sea is the victory song that Moses and the Israelites sang after crossing the Red Sea. The prayer is an affirmation of the Jew's belief in God's role in history, and is recited while standing each and every morning as part of the preliminary service. At the conclusion of the Song of the Sea there are two verses that are added on, taken from the Books of the Minor Prophets Obadiah and Zechariah, respectively:

And saviors will come up on Mount Zion to judge
the Mount of Esau, and the kingdom shall be the
Lord's. (Obadiah 1:21)

And the Lord shall be King over all the earth, and
in that day the Lord shall be One, and His Name
shall be One. (Zechariah 14:9).

The Book of Obadiah denounces the unbrotherly
and cruel conduct of the Edomites in the day of
Israel's ruin, when Jerusalem was destroyed by the
Babylonians. Other nations in later times played
the cruel role of Edom and manifested wanton
hatred toward Israel. In this verse, Obadiah predicts Israel's triumph over them all: "saviours will
climb Mount Zion," and there will be no more
senseless hatred between nation and nation.

The Prophet Zechariah roused the exiles who had
returned from Babylon from their despondency
and led them in the rebuilding of the Temple. The
wonderful saying that appears in the liturgy pro-
fesses the Messianic hope of Judaism and the
spiritual goal of human history, namely, that in the
future there will be a universal recognition of
God's sovereignty. God's manifold revelations of
Himself shall be acknowledged by all to be merely
aspects of the one sole Name by which God made
Himself known to Israel. This is one of the fundamental verses of the Jewish conception of the
Kingdom of Heaven. It proclaims the Providential
care of God for all humankind and the future
recognition of the true God by all humankind. The
verse also closes all services and appears as the
concluding verse of the prayer the *Aleynu.*

Kedusha (Sanctification)

The *Kedusha* is one of the liturgical prayers that is restricted to congregational worship, requiring a quorum of ten adults for its recital. It is attached to the *Amidah* prayer in the morning and afternoon service.

The threefold repetition of the words "Holy, Holy, Holy" (*kadosh, kadosh, kadosh*) are taken from the Book of Isaiah 6:3 and denotes emphasis and intensity. The introductory words of the *Kedusha* itself summon the congregation to join in the praise of God in the manner of angelic hosts, who keep calling to one another: "Holy, Holy, Holy is the Lord of Hosts, the whole earth is filled with God's Presence." (Note: This threefold utterance of "Holy, Holy, Holy" is also included in the prayer *uva L'Tzion*, which is called *Kedusha d'sidrah*, because, according to the commentator Rashi, it is inserted in the daily minimal biblical lesson designed for all of Israel.)

A second verse appears in the *Kedusha*, which is taken from the Book of Ezekiel 3:12: "Blessed be the Presence of God in His place." This verse, recited by the congregation, is the response to the threefold repetition of the words "Holy, Holy, Holy." The verse implies that all that is sublime in nature and history is the outward expression and radiation of God's power.

Anenu Paragraph for Fast Days

On fast days in the Jewish calendar, a special paragraph beginning with the word *anenu*—"answer
us"—is recited. In this prayer the worshiper asks
that God answer us and hear our cry. Embedded in
this prayer is a verse based in a verse in the Book
of Isaiah 65:24: "Before we call to You, answer us."

The Eighth Blessing of the *Amidah*—
Blessing for Healing

This blessing is based on a verse in the Book of
Jeremiah 17:14: "Heal me, Lord, and let me be
healed." In the verse that appears in the *Amidah*,
the liturgist changed the Jeremiah verse from the
singular to the plural form. It is a petition for
healing to all who are sick: "Heal us, O God, and we
shall be healed." This is in keeping with the spirit
of most of the prayers in the prayerbook, which are
written in the plural form to include all of the
people of Israel.

Tachanun

The *Tachanun* supplication, recited on weekdays
after the *Amidah* prayer, is often referred to as
nefilat appayim ("falling on the face") because in

the early days of the Talmud it was customary to recite it in the form of prostration with the face to the ground. It contains heart-stirring elegies and supplications, giving voice to the sufferings of the Jewish people over many centuries.

Three verses from the Books of the Prophets are included in the *Tachanan* prayers. The first is from the Book of Jeremiah 14:7, "Though our sins testify against us, act, O God, for the sake of Your name."

The second is from the Book of Isaiah 64:7, "And now, God, You are our Father; we are the clay and You are our Potter, we are the work of Your hands."

The final verse in the *Tachanun* prayer is taken from the Book of Joel 2:17, "Wherefore should they say among the peoples, Where is their God?"

This verse is a favorite taunt of Israel's enemies. The implication is that since the Israelites claim to be God's people, why does God not save them in their misfortune? God cannot forsake His people, for then He would betray His own cause.

Yehi Ratzon: May It Be Your Will

The end of the *Amidah* was accounted an appropriate place for silent individual prayer. The *Amidah* concludes with a prayer to God for the rebuilding of the Temple in Jerusalem. This is followed by a verse from the Book of Malachi 3:4: "Then the offering of Judah and Jerusalem shall be pleasing to God as in the days of yore and in the years of old."

Introductory Prayer to Torah Service

When the Ark is opened and the Torah is about to be removed from the Ark, two verses are recited from the Book of Numbers 10:35–36: "And it came to pass, when the Ark set forward, that Moses said, Rise up, O God, and Your enemies shall be scattered, and they that hate You shall flee before You."

These verses constitute the invocation prayer of the children of Israel in the wilderness, whenever the Ark of the Covenant went forward. The Ark of the Covenant, guiding the Israelite tribes in their desert wanderings, typified God in front of His people— the Divine Presence—protecting them and leading them to victory. These verses are then followed by the following well-known verse from the Book of Isaiah 2:3: "For out of Zion shall go forth the Torah, and the word of God from Jerusalem."

These words are taken from the prophet's sublime vision of the Messianic age, when Israel's spiritual teachings shall extend to all humanity and dominate the hearts of people.

Va'anachnu lo neyda—As for Us, We Do Not Know

This prayer follows the prayer *Shomer Yisrael*— guardian of Israel. It is a shortened form of the *Tachanun* supplicatory prayers, originally created for latecomers. Like the longer *Tachanun*, the worshiper asks for God's grace and kindness. It also has one verse from the Book of the Prophet Habakkuk 3:2: "In wrath, remember to be merciful." In executing retribution against the arrogant enemy, the worshiper petitions that God may have pity on the distress of His people.

Uva L'Tzion Goel A Redeemer Shall Come to Zion

Pious worshipers of old desired to close their morning prayers with readings and expositions from the Books of the Prophets, in the same manner that the *Haftarah*, originally a prophetical lesson, closed the Sabbath and Festival Morning service. Stress of life, however, compelled the abbreviating of these daily readings. In the prayer *uva l'Tzion Goel*, this daily prophetical lesson consists merely of Isaiah 59:20–21:

> And a redeemer shall come to Zion and unto them that turn from transgression in Jacob, says God. And as for Me, this is My covenant with them, said the Lord: My spirit that is upon you, and My words which I have put in your mouth, shall not depart out of your mouth, nor out of the mouth of your seed, nor out of the mouth of your seed's seed, says the Lord, from henceforth and forever.

These two verses contain a promise of redemption, as well as an assurance of an everlasting covenant that will link the generations in the sacred resolve to preserve both the spirit and the letter of God's revelation to Israel.

Following these verses is the sanctification, consisting of verses from Isaiah 6:3 and Ezekiel 3:12:

> And one cried to another and said: Holy, Holy, Holy is the Lord of Hosts, the whole world is filled with God's Presence.

> Then a wind lifted me up and I heard behind me the voice of a great rushing saying, Blessed be the glory of God from His place.

As the repetition of the sanctification is merely the accompaniment of a private biblical exposition (called the *kedusha de'Sidra*), it is not recited congregationally, but by each worshiper individually for himself or herself.

Several additional verses appear at the conclusion of this prayer, one from the Book of Micah 7:20 and the other from the Book of the Prophet Jeremiah 17:7. "You will show faithfulness to Jacob and lovingkindness to Abraham, as You have sworn unto our ancestors from the days of old." Here, God's promise to the patriarchs is the ground of both the appeal to God's mercy and the confidence that the appeal will be heeded.

The second verse is from the Book of Jeremiah 17:7. "Blessed is the man that trusts in God, and whose trust the Lord is."

The final verses are Isaiah 26:4 and Isaiah 42:21, "Trust in the Lord forever, for the Lord is God, an everlasting Rock" and "The Lord was pleased for

His righteousness' sake, to make the teaching great and glorious." Here the sense is that the Torah embraces Divine revelation and moral instruction to Israel, who is to be the appointed messenger for propagating its truth to all people and thus render the Torah great and glorious.

Kaddish

There are several different forms of the *Kaddish* prayer. The opening words of all of them—*yitgadal veyitkadash*, "magnified and sanctified be God's Name"—are said to have been inspired by the prophet Ezekiel's vision of a time when God will become great and hallowed in the eyes of all the nations (Ezekiel 38:23).

Aleynu

The *Aleynu* prayer was originally part of the additional *Musaf* service for Rosh Hashanah. For about the last six hundred years, it has been included at the end of prayer services in the synagogue.

The second paragraph of the *Aleynu* has a universalistic theme. It concludes with a verse from the Prophet Zechariah (14:9), envisioning a time in the future when everyone in the world will acknowledge God as the One and Only: ". . . on that day the Lord shall be One and His name shall be One."

Yigdal

The liturgical poem *Yigdal*, used as a closing hymn, was said to have been composed by Rabbi Daniel ben Yehudah of fourteenth-century Rome. It consists of thirteen lines that summarize the thirteen principles of faith as formulated by Moses Maimonides in his *Mishneh* commentary (*Sanhedrin* 10:1). Principles 6, 7, and 8 all relate to prophecy and Moses. Principle number 6 states that "all the prophets are true." Principle 7 states that "Moses was the greatest of all the prophets." Principle number 8 states that "the entire Torah was divinely given to Moses."

22

The High Holy Day *Machzor*

In addition to the previously enumerated references there are also a number of special prophetic verses that appear exclusively in the prayerbook for the High Holy Days, used for recitation on Rosh Hashanah and Yom Kippur.

Three sections of the *Musaf* additional service, known as the *Malchuyot* (God's Kingship), *Zichronot* (Remembrance), and *Shofarot* (Rams' Horns) deal with the themes of God the King, God the Divine Recorder, and God the Revealer of our Law. The *Mishnah Rosh Hashanah* (4:6), compiled in the second century of the Common Era, already mentions these three divisions as part of the ritual of the day. It refers to the practice, still observed, of sounding the ram's horn between each portion, and the provision that each of these three sections contain not less than ten verses from the threefold division of the Bible—the Five Books of Moses, the Sacred Writings, and the Prophets.

The following verses from the Books of the Prophets appear in each of these three sections.

243

Malchuyot Sovereignty Verses

1. Thus says the Lord of Hosts, King and Redeemer of Israel: "I am the first, and I am the last, and besides Me there is no God" (Isaiah 44:6).

2. And redeemers shall ascend Mount Zion to judge Mount Esau and the sovereignty shall be the Lord's (Obadiah 1:21).

3. And the Lord shall be King over all the earth; on that day the Lord shall be One and His name one (Zechariah 14:9).

Zichronot Remembrance Verses

1. Go and proclaim so that Jerusalem may hear: Thus says the Lord, "I remember for you the devotion of your youth, the love of your espousals; how you went after Me in the wilderness, in a land unsown" (Jeremiah 2:2).

2. Nevertheless I will remember My covenant with you in the days of your youth; and I will establish unto you an everlasting covenant (Ezekiel 16:60).

3. Is not Ephraim My beloved son, My beloved child, for even when I speak against him, I remember him with affection. Therefore, My heart yearns for him; yea, I will surely have compassion upon him, says the Lord (Jeremiah 31:20).

Shofarot Trumpet Verses

1. All you inhabitants of the world and dwellers on the earth; when a banner is lifted up on the mountain, see you, and when the *shofar* is sounded, hear (Isaiah 18:3).

2. The Lord shall be revealed unto them, and His arrows go forth as lightning. God shall sound the *shofar*, and shall go in the whirlwinds of the south (Zechariah 9:14).

For Further Reading

Blank, Sheldon. *Understanding the Prophets*. New York: Union of American Hebrew Congregations, 1969.

Buber, Martin. *I and Thou*. New York: Scribner, 1958.

Cohen, Beryl D. *The Prophets: Their Personalities and Teachings*. New York: Bloch Publishers, 1960.

Halevi, Judah. *The Kuzari*. New York: Schocken Books, 1964.

Heschel, Abraham J. *Prophetic Inspiration after the Prophets. Maimonides and Other Medieval Authorities*. Ed., Morris M. Fairstein. New Jersey: Ktav, 1996.

———. *The Prophets*. Philadelphia: Jewish Publications, 1962.

Maimonides, Moses. *Guide of the Perplexed*. Translated by Shlomo Pines. Chicago: University of Chicago Press, 1963.

Plaut, Gunther, ed. *The Haftarah Commentary*. New York: Union of American Hebrew Congregations, 1996.

Smith, J. M. Powis, and William A. Irwin. *The Prophets and Their Times*. Chicago: University of Chicago Press, 1941.

Wollman-Tsamir, Pinchas, ed. *Graphic History of the Jewish Heritage*. New York: Shengold Publishers, 1963.

Index

major concepts and
teachings, 159–160
modern interpreta-
tions, 162
notable quotations,
162
in rabbinic literature,
160–161
synopsis, 158
Jonah, Rabbi, repeating
prophecy of prede-
cessors, 44
Jonathan, Rabbi, 36
Joshua, 29, 42, 66, 129
Josiah, King, 104
Judah, Rabbi
boastfulness, 56
Moses compared to
other prophets,
43–44
Judah, Rav, 128
justice, 194

Kaddish, Book of Ezekiel
in, 241
Kedusha (sanctification),
235
Kimchi, 82, 191
kindness, 168, 194
Kingdom of God, 185
Korcha, Rabbi Joshua
ben, 200
Megillah, 56–57
Kuzari, The (Halevi), 223

Lakish, Resh, 56
Lamentations, Book of,
117
lands, suitability of
Israel versus other
for Divine revela-
tions, 53–54, 61
language
full/half speech, 50,
52, 61 (*See also*
speech)
power of, 35
of prophets, 19–20
strength of, 59
of themes, 41, 60
"Later Prophets," 164
legal decisions, Jewish,
23
lessons, regarding
prophecy, 59–61
Levi, Rabbi, ambiguity
of prophecy of na-
tions of the world,
52–53
listening, importance of,
18
lists of prophets. *See*
prophets, lists of
literary prophets, 13–16,
19
after the days of, 23
list and summary of,
14–16

About the Author

Rabbi Ronald Isaacs is the spiritual leader of Temple Sholom in Bridgewater, New Jersey. He received his doctorate in instructional technology from Columbia University's Teacher's College. He is the author of numerous books, including *Loving Companions: Our Jewish Wedding Album*, co-authored with Leora Isaacs. Rabbi Isaacs currently serves on the editorial board of *Shofar* Magazine and is a member of the Publications Committee of the Rabbinical Assembly. He resides in New Jersey with his wife, Leora, and their children, Keren and Zachary.